JOHN KNOX

JOHN KNOX

A Quatercentenary Reappraisal

Lectures given at the University of Edinburgh on the four hundredth anniversary of the death of John Knox

Edited by

DUNCAN SHAW

THE SAINT ANDREW PRESS
EDINBURGH

First published in 1975 by
THE SAINT ANDREW PRESS
121 George Street, Edinburgh EH2 4YN

© The Saint Andrew Press 1975

ISBN 0 7152 0246 4

Printed in Great Britain by
T. & A. Constable Ltd, Edinburgh.

To

The Very Reverend Henry C. Whitley, Ph.D., D.D., minister of the High Kirk of Edinburgh, 1954–72 and Convener of the General Assembly's Committee for the Commemoration of the Fourth Centenary of the death of John Knox. A successor of John Knox not only as a minister at Edinburgh but as a Watchman and a Trumpet of the Lord.

PREFACE

The lectures are printed almost exactly as they were delivered in the University of Edinburgh during the commemoration of the four hundredth anniversary of the death of John Knox.

Thanks are expressed to Dr Harry Whitley whose vigour and vision inspired the commemoration, to the lecturers whose participation and co-operation made publication possible and to Dr J. B. Barclay of the University of Edinburgh for his part in making it a memorable academic occasion.

Duncan Shaw

Edinburgh

CONTENTS

ABBREVIATIONS

Cal. S.P. Scot. *Calendar of the State Papers relating to Scotland and Mary, Queen of Scots, 1547–1603,* edited by J. Bain and others. Edinburgh, 1898–1969. 13 vols.

Knox, *History* *John Knox's History of the Reformation in Scotland,* edited by W. C. Dickinson. Edinburgh, 1949. 2 vols.

Knox, *Works* *The Works of John Knox,* collected and edited by D. Laing. Edinburgh, 1846–64. 6 vols.

S.H.R. *The Scottish Historical Review.* Glasgow, 1904–28, vols. i–xxv; Edinburgh, 1948–65, vols. xxvi–xliv; and Aberdeen, 1966f., vols. xlvf.

NOTE

The quotations from Knox's writings and other sixteenth-century sources have been modernised in the printed lectures apart from that of Mr Murison.

The Europe of John Knox

The Reverend Professor E. G. Rupp, F.B.A., D.D.

Dixie Professor of Ecclesiastical History,
University of Cambridge

In the heart of Paris there are two memorials of Napoleon. The one, in the War Museum of the Invalides, shows Napoleon's shabby blue serge, immortal hat, surrounded by the massed standards, torn and stained, of the regiments of France. A few hundred yards away is the tomb of Napoleon, grandiose in its green and brown stone, its deep vault flanked by the monuments of the Marshals of the Empire. On the one hand the Napoleon of history, vulnerable, poignant, moving: on the other the public image, the myth. Something like that seems to happen to religious leaders, to the founders of great confessions: to the Lutheran Luther, the Calvinist Calvin, the Methodist Wesley. A fourth centenary seems a good time to put the historians to work, to ask 'Will the real John Knox stand up?'

I am no political historian: it is Professor Denys Hay who is the authority on this concept of 'Europe'—as it emerges from the older view of the mediaeval unity of Christendom. He finds a significant moment in the letter which the humanist Pope Pius II wrote to Mehemet the conqueror of Constantinople:

> We cannot believe that you are unaware of the resources of the Christian peoples, how strong is Spain, how war-like France, how numerous are the peoples of Germany, how powerful Britain, how bold Poland, how vigorous Hungary, how rich and spirited and skilled in warfare is Italy.[1]

It is proper, then to talk of Europe in connection with the emerging society of the sixteenth century. But there is a sense in which, as Federico Chabod suggested, Europe comes of age only in the eighteenth century: Europe of artists, sciences, academies, philosophers, Newton, Locke, Galileo, Corneille, Racine, Goethe;

[1] D. Hay, *Europe: the emergence of an idea* (rev. ed.). Edinburgh, 1968. 83–84.

I

that Europe of which Burke could say in 1796 'no European can be a complete exile in any part of it'.[1]

Perhaps between 'Christendom' and 'Europe' we should interpose a transition period and another concept, that of the 'Christian Nations': for in this period, one nation after another, like characters at the end of a pantomime, take their bow one by one, hold for a moment the focused limelight, each the bearer of a Christian culture distinctive and separate—Portugal and Spain, England, Holland, Sweden, France, Germany, Russia.[2] This is not unrelated to what we may call the device of geographical expostulation in the preaching of John Knox and the Edwardian preachers in England—their concern to address a Christian Nation—'O England!' 'O Scotland!'

But these overall concepts damage if they blur the facts of the changing empirical situation across the West in the sixteenth century, of which the most obvious are the deep continuities with the mediaeval world. The continuing three-dimensional great game between the Pope, the Emperor and the King of France, the bedevilling of Italy by it, the conflicting interests of great families, the Habsburgs and the Valois and the Guises: the Medici and the Farnese. Within the Catholic world, the two conflicting axes of political power: that of Philip II in Spain, involved in the affairs of Holland and so of England: that of the policies of the Guises in France, so fateful for Scotland and so for England too. There was the cautious empiricism of some popes from ancient diplomatic wariness, and the hard won canniness of the Emperor Charles V, as he tried to moderate or slow down the doctrinaire impatience of religious dévots like Mary Tudor or the Cardinal Pole. Within the Catholic and Protestant world there were so many diverse and conflicting interests, all in a crisis playing their own hand, that even the ablest statesmen were as mariners peering doubtfully ahead into a fog from which might

---

[1] John Foxe's extraordinary play *Christus Triumphans*, Basle, 1556, includes in its cast 'Ecclesia' who is the mother of 'Europus' and 'Africa'.

[2] The thought of Britain as an Elect Nation in Spenser and Foxe and of God's own Englishman in Milton can be paralleled in Spain and Portugal (cf. J. H. Parry, *The Spanish Seaborne Empire*. London, 1966: C. R. Boxer, *The Dutch Seaborne Empire, 1415–1825*. London, 1969). The only difference seems to be between nations which needed to assert this and those which take it for granted, as France has done from the time of Joan of Arc to General de Gaulle.

loom at any moment disaster. In Germany a high tide of
Lutheranism seemed to have been reached, an alignment of cities
and principalities against their Catholic opponents which reached
but a temporary halt in 1559. Well might William Burghley
commend 'the example of Denmark' as an instance of a crown
able to grasp and settle the issues of the episcopate and of church
property, but neither in Scotland nor England in the 1550s could
any force be strong enough to do what Henry VIII had failed to
do in the first years of the Reformation.

Some day somebody will write an essay on 'Time and the
Reformation' for the historical scene resembles a Dickensian image
of a shop full of clocks all chiming and striking and whirring at
different moments, going at different speeds. One needs to note
the slowing up and acceleration of the Reformation and the
different causes of it (e.g., the slowing down of Lutheranism in
German cities after 1524 and the outbreak of the eucharistic
controversy). It is always important to bear in mind in the case
of England, the ten-year gap, the fact in England 1527 is a key
date compared with 1517 on the Continent. And by the 1540s
this means that what happened in England and Scotland was
affected by a whole spate of argument and happening, in the
presence of a great literature of liturgical and theological change.
When in the 1550s there came the appeal to violence and the
outbreak of popular iconoclasticism, it is worth remembering that
it was as long ago as 1526 that in St Gall the 'rascal multitude'
brushed aside the godly magistrate in the person of Vadianus
and destroyed the images of the great abbey.

More significant is the change of mood between the 1520s and
the 1550s. If one cannot quite say of Germany in 1525 'bliss was
it in that dawn to be alive', yet there is a zest and hopefulness
about the German Reformation, a confident belief that the Word
would go on triumphantly to finish what had been so astonishingly
begun. The bitter polemic of the ageing Luther shows how much
things had changed by 1545—the slowing down of the pace of
Lutheran reform; the achievement of the Papal Council; the fact
that it had met at all; the obvious military resurgence of the
Imperial power. Now Luther begins to quote more and more
from Daniel and Revelation, and in Knox's writings, and not
least in the Scots Confession, there is an apocalyptic undertone, a
new sense of the collision between the true and false church and

the appearance of anti-Christ: and these things are no longer left
to the crackpot left of the radical sects. The Reformers had no
sooner begun to expound the *jus reformandi* of the godly magistrate
when they faced the problem of resistance to the ungodly ruler
and the old tension evident in Luther between Romans 13 and
Acts 5:29 gave way to an attempt to bring the Old Testament
prophets into the argument. Apocalyptic seems to recur in those
moments in history when things come to the boil, and when a
spiral view of historical development replaces the linear one of
calmer days: in those periods when the sleeping volcano under-
lying human existence erupts, violence is in the air, and the
irrational takes over. Such was Europe in the 1550s on the edge
of the terrible period of religious war.

In a classic essay, F. W. Maitland showed the critical importance
of the years when the Reformation in Scotland hung in the
balance, not only for Scotland but for the fate of England, and the
whole issue of the success of the Counter-Reformation. In these
months, John Knox was of vital importance: there was nobody
else with like moral courage and integrity, none other of whom
it could be written,

> the voice of one man is able in one hour to put more life in us
> than five hundred trumpets continually blustering in our ears.[1]

It came to be of immense importance that John Knox knew what
was happening from the inside, from his own experiences in
France and in Switzerland. We first meet him as that Erasmian
figure, a tutor with his bairns at their lessons, though in the
grim context of that Cave of Adullam, the Castle of St Andrews.
But the rest of the story resembles Erasmus only in the frequency
and extent of his travels. Knox marched towards the sound of the
guns, Erasmus away from them. He made repeated journeys
across the Counter-Reformation strip between Italy and Spain
and France across which even Cardinal Pole could not pass without peril—when he might easily have remained peacefully in
Geneva. He had Huguenot friends and correspondents, almost
agents, and one would like to know much more about the cloak
and dagger side of Knox's career about which there are many
hints and one or two revealing incidents.

At his listening post in Dieppe, on uncomfortable lonely

[1] *Cal. S.P. Scot.*, i. No. 1017.

journeys by horse and waggon, on the high seas overhearing treasonable gossip or poking into suspicious contraband in the hold, he did not miss much of what was going on at the court of France and he was even more aware of the growing tension in the countryside: from the violence at Vassy and Amboise to the final horror of St Bartholomew which confirmed his direct prophecies. Hence his fury at compromise and the fierceness of his denunciation of apostasy from the good cause. Nor may we underrate the importance for him of England: his love-hate relationship with England and the English crown. His love for England: one would give much for the full story of that curious sabbatical leave to see his sons, while in Scotland the whole climactic tragedy of Kirk o' Field and the dire aftermath convulsed the nation. That, a few days after his death, his sons, Nathanael and Eliezer—revealing names—were entered in St John's College, Cambridge bespeaks softened relations with the Bowes family, a sense of the perils of Scotland for the bearers of his name, but something more; a respect and affection for England where once or twice he might have settled. And the core of his own ministry was not, perhaps, in those amazing concentrated tours of Scotland but amid the congregations at Berwick, Newcastle, the Thames Valley, and that too short interlude in Edwardian London, the only time he was ever seriously tempted to take his ease in Zion. It is this wider background, penetratingly interpreted, seen through the periscope of the Old Testament prophets, which undergirds his prophesying. No wonder that he had a nose for trouble and could smell disaster from afar.

So much for the outer world. What of the inner man? We may say of John Knox, as has been said of Martin Luther and of Thomas Müntzer, that he was 'wholly a preacher, wholly a theologian'. Not, as he protested, an academic—'Consider, Brethren, it is no speculative Theolog which desireth to give you courage'—and he deliberately chose the ephemeral impact of the living word as preferable to the vain attempt to 'compose books for the age to come'.[1] But theologian in the sense of Luther's existential cry, 'Not reading or speculating, but living, dying and being damned make a theologian'. I want to give at this point a short table of Knox's spiritual and theological affinities with other Reformers and with the earlier Reformations.

[1] Knox, *Works*, iii. 10: vi. 229.

There may be between men a relation of pedigree—as a Raphael or a Giorgione may depend on a great succession going back through a Masaccio to Giotto. Here there is a direct debt: an acknowledged transmission. Such a relation of pedigree there is between John Knox and John Calvin. But there may also be a relationship of spiritual affinity. We are familiar in science with the way, say in atomic research, investigators in different places, but using the same tools and with similar presuppositions, facing similar problems may come up with similar results. The claim that 'so and so' or 'somebody else' really 'split the atom' resembles the argument between Zwingli and Luther about who first re-discovered justification by only faith. The truth is that with the new humanist tools turned on Biblical theology, exploring the Pauline material against a lopsided legalism in the church around, there was bound to be this phenomenon of simultaneous dis-covery. So that if Knox has a fairly direct relationship to the teaching of Calvin and of Beza, he has a remarkable spiritual affinity with many strands in the Reformation outside the Reformed tradition.

The obvious physical differences between Martin Luther and John Knox ought not to hide some temperamental similarities. If, as Chesterton said, inside every fat man there is a little thin man trying to get out, then outside every little thin man there may be a fat man trying to get in, and so spirits blend. Both had immense moral courage, and in the pulpit were fearless. But they were not temperamentally brave and there are obvious and recurrent timidities. Luther at Augsburg in 1518 and at Worms in 1521, Knox in St Andrews in 1547 and again and again in the period 1559–65 stood firm and enabled others to do so. But they did not enjoy danger. Knox has been accused by some, because he half accused himself, of cowardice in the face of the enemy when he went into exile from England in the beginning of Mary Tudor's reign. But just as Karl Barth, who was Swiss, could honourably withdraw from the German Church struggle, so Knox stayed in England until beyond the point of danger, and could thereafter have remained quietly and peacefully in Geneva all his days had not the plight of his country drawn him. Yes, I think we may say he marched towards the sound of the guns even if we have to add 'with butterflies in his stomach'.

Both had what C. S. Lewis calls the power of rebuking magnificently which produces great polemic. Both had a talent for indiscretion which paid off, but which thoroughly scared their friends at court—as a comparison of George Spalatin's letters about Luther with ambassador Thomas Randolph's about Knox plainly show. Both had more sense of humour than all the rest of the Reformers put together. Above all Knox knew what Luther gave to the Reformation, the meaning of *Anfechtung*, that temptation which strikes the jugular vein of faith. Those who have written most perceptively about Knox—Lord Eustace Percy and Pierre Janton—have told us that the secret of Knox is to be found in the inward man, in his prayers. Knox and Luther knew that there are heights and depths of anguish in the good fight of faith.

'I know,' says Knox, 'how hard the battle is . . . I know the anger, wrath, and indignation which it conceiveth against God, calling all his promises in doubt, and being ready every hour utterly to fall from God . . . Against which rests only faith, . . . wherein if we continue our most desparate calamities shall he turn to gladness, and to a prosperous end.'[1]

Knox's *Declaration of the True Nature and Object of Prayer* is an unpretentious plain tract which may include commonplaces of contemporary spirituality, but it has some fine stuff in it and many points of contact with Luther's equally lucid *Letter to Peter the Barber on how to Pray*. In both, temptation and the fight of faith are anchored on the never-failing promises of God. In 1548 Knox published an abridgement of a treatise on *Justification* by Henry Balnaves, the Scottish lawyer who was a prisoner in Rouen while Knox lay in the French galleys off the coast. Knox's abridgement answered the need he felt for simple plain catechetical material for ordinary people. But it does scant justice to Balnaves' remarkable work, a compendium as it is of Christian doctrine, setting justification by faith within the design of God for human salvation, with a doctrine of the Church grounded in election, and an exposition of civil righteousness and the doctrine of vocation. It has been suggested by Dr Hugh Watt that in the making of it Balnaves drew upon Luther's *Commentary on Galatians*. But there are evident similarities to Luther's *Preface to the Romans*, and this raises the possibility that Balnaves did not read Luther at first hand but knew him through the writings of William Tyndale.

[1] Knox, *Works*, iii. 101–2.

Balnaves' treatise is not only Lutheran: it reminds us of the
Rhineland treatises of the 1520s, of Martin Bucer and Henry of
Ulm and Cellarius's *De operibus Dei*, 1527, where justification by
faith is similarly set in a view of election and predestination which
is not Lutheran, and which suggests we have still much to learn
about the repercussions of late mediaeval Augustinianism, within
orthodoxy and from the Waldensian, Hussite and Lollard sects.

Luther and Knox had great and notable stresses in their preaching in common. Both emphasised the 'once for all'ness of the
offer of the gospel to nations. Luther expressed this in a famous and
lovely passage,

> Buy, dear people, while the fair is at the door. Gather in the
> harvest while it is sunshine and fair weather. For know this,
> that God's Word is as a passing shower which does not return
> where once it has been. . . .

Knox too did not believe that men and nations have indefinite
last chances.

> Most evident it is that where the light of God's Word for the
> unthankfulness of men has been taken away that there it is not
> to this day restored again. Witness whole Israel and all the
> countries of the Gentiles where the apostles first preached.
> What is in Asia? What in Africa? Abnegation of the very
> Saviour. What in those most notable churches of the Grecians
> where Jesus Christ was planted by Paul and long after watered
> by others? Mahomet and his false sect . . . and shall he spare
> us if we are unthankful yea, if we be worse nor they were?

And in another place:

> The sun keepeth his ordinary course and starteth not back from
> the West to the South: but when it goeth down we lack light
> of the same until it rise again the next day . . . so it is with the
> light of the gospel which has its day appointed wherein it
> shines to realms and nations. If it be condemned, darkness
> follows.

Like the first Christians, Knox lived in a world where 'martyr'
and 'apostate' were a grim polarity, even though it might be
a gradual apostasy of little compromises by men moved by the
universal self-interest, Shakespeare's 'tickling commodity'. Knox

in the reign of Mary could never forgive those who had turned their back, and kept his worst invective for the Laird of Grange and Maitland of Lethington because these men had once been his comrades and had become the Mr Facing Both Ways and the Mr By Ends of the Scottish Reformation who might have been its Mr Standfast and its Valiant for Truth.

For both Luther and for Knox, the passage in Ezekiel 33:9 was to be taken in deadly seriousness. Here was outlined their prophet vocation as Watchman, their duty to warn the nation at all costs, with the admonition that if they failed they would be partakers of the sin and judgment of which they had failed to warn. Not that Knox and Luther had affinity only on their sterner side. It is important that both were not only Paul men but John men: Luther's great course of sermons on St John's Gospel in his middle years sums up a most important facet of his thought and not least of his Christology, while St John was Knox's safe, sure anchorage in every dark and dangerous hour. To it both Luther and Knox turned in the *Stündlein* of death.

In the cities of Switzerland, there arose an un-Lutheran pattern of Reformation, not unrelated to the community life of their civic background, but there were differences and tensions between the theology and life-style of Zürich, Berne, Basel, Geneva which perhaps were bridged by the Consensus Tigurinus in 1549 and the close relation between Bullinger and Beza thereafter. There is no relation of pedigree but there are obvious affinities with Zwingli. At the heart of Knox's religion, as of Zwingli's, there is obedience, devotion to the one whom both love to call 'my Captain Christ'. Both dabbled in military history and Zwingli's *Plan for a military campaign* shows that he would have read with interest Knox's vivid battle pieces like that of Cupar Muir. Both dreamed of a great alliance of Reformed cities and nations, and became willy nilly and perhaps more willy than nilly, involved in military ploys. For both, the prophet Isaiah was of importance as a statesman holding up before a nation the Word of God. Knox's great sermon on Isaiah 21 follows the expository method which Zwingli had launched in the Gross Münster forty years before, of following through a passage breaking the text in pieces, feeding the flock with the bread of life.

And when Zwingli's mutilated body lay on the field of Cappel, a Catholic soldier muttered over it—'A rotten heretic, but a damned good Swiss'—and none of Knox's foes ever doubted his patriotism. Oecolampadius of Basel was more than an echo of his Zürich ally. This was shown in his oration in 1531 on *Excommunication*, dealing with the problem of discipline which was to exercise the Reformers for the next half-century. Zwingli's views were perhaps too prophylactically oriented, concerned to preserve the church unspotted from the church, whereas Oecolampadius was concerned with the pastoral office of winning back the penitent. His blueprint for discipline included the emphasis on the brotherly admonition and on the use of lay elders which was adapted by Bucer with his Kirchenpfleger at Strasbourg and so became, through Calvin, an element in the Scottish order. We are perhaps only at the beginning of Bullinger studies, but Bullinger's Zürich in the 1540s provided a pattern of reformed churchmanship and godly discipline which influenced Britain by means of a stream of young students going to Edwardian England, while it was from Zürich that John Hooper drew his doctrine, the Edwardian bishop who temperamentally stood nearest to John Knox. Bullinger's doctrine of predestination[1] is complex and shows some signs of modification and development and I should not be competent to compare his teaching with that which Knox enunciated in his own treatise. But though Knox is plainly and explicitly the debtor to John Calvin, his major preoccupation in writing his study was to combat the Anabaptists who were represented at the court of Edward VI. And it is Zwingli and then Bullinger in Zürich who first turned to the doctrine of Predestination as a controversial weapon against the Anabaptists: for by so doing they cut the ground from under the feet of the radical argument by shifting the ground from the appeal to experience, from justification and saving faith, and even from the argument about baptism, to the design of God for men's salvation in Christ before the foundation of the world. Calvin was for Knox a friend and ally and patron, the one to whom he turned again and again for practical and theological advice, which he by no means always took, while it was quite advisedly that he did not give Calvin a preview of his *First Blast of the Trumpet against the monstrous regiment of Women*. It was to Geneva that Knox came to find peace after the bitter Frankfurt troubles and to Geneva that he drew his

[1] Cf. P. Walser, *Die Prädestination bei Heinrich Bullinger*. Zürich, 1957.

friends, as he wrote to Anne Locke, 'Where I neither fear nor am ashamed to say is the most perfect school of Christ that ever was in the earth since the days of the apostles. In other places, I confess Christ to be truly preached; but manners and religion so sincerely reformed, I have not yet seen in any other place.'[1]

Three years later, when she was at Geneva and he was back in Britain, his letters to her were as much concerned with books as with gossip. 'Many things I have which I would have required for myself, namely, Calvin upon Isaiah, and his Institutions revised. . . . If ye can find the means to send me the books . . . I will provide that ye shall receive the prices.'[2]

After the death of Calvin, Knox wrote often to Beza letters which have mostly disappeared, keeping him up to date with Scottish affairs, giving news which Beza passed on to Bullinger.

The discovery that Knox's 'accomplished female friend', as the Victorian poet had it, was the daughter of the English merchant Stephen Vaughan is of great interest since it links Knox with the beginnings of the English Reformation and with the circle around William Tyndale.[3] For Stephen Vaughan was the government intermediary with Tyndale and obviously well instructed in Tyndale and his relationships though he could characteristically disavow being at any stage a Tyndalian or a Martinian. But there is an evident connection of both with the Merchants' House at Antwerp where Tyndale, Rogers and others of the English Reformers were chaplains, and Anne's husband Henry Locke was one of these English merchants who had dealings with Antwerp. This is a link with congregations in London with which Knox was associated, and I cannot doubt there is a real pedigree of association between him and those who had personal memories of the Bible groups in London denounced by Sir Thomas More and attended by such devout laymen as Humphrey Monmouth, one

---

[1] 9 December 1556 (Knox, *op. cit.*, iv. 240).

[2] November 1559 (*ibid.*, vi. 101). Again, February 1560, 'If ye can find a messenger, I heartily pray you to send me the books for which I wrote you before' (*ibid.* vi, 108).

[3] G. R. Elton, *Reform and Renewal*. London, 1973: L. Lupton, *The History of the Geneva Bible*. London, 1972, iii: P. Collinson, 'The Role of Women in the English Reformation illustrated by the Life and Friendships of Anne Locke', in *Studies in Church History*, ed. G. J. Cuming. London, 1965, ii. 258–72 (this interesting essay does not go into the Knox-Locke correspondence in depth).

of Tyndale's patrons. Anne Locke was one of the group of godly
blue-stockings of the English Reformation which begins with
the ladies around Anne Boleyn and which later includes Anne
Askew, Catherine Parr, Lady Jane Grey, who have in recent
days been claimed as Erasmian. But about the only adjective
nobody has ever applied to John Knox is that he was an Erasmian
and I do not doubt that most of the women described by Dr
McConica as such, were in effect also Protestant Reformers. At
any rate it was to Anne Locke that Knox really let his hair down,
and it is his letters to her that have the inside news, the top secret
gossip which supplements and sometimes outwrites Knox's
History of the Reformation.

> We do nothing but go about Jericho, blowing with trumpets,
> as God giveth strength, hoping victory by his power alone.
> Christ Jesus is preached even in Edinburgh and his blessed
> sacraments rightly ministered in all congregations where the
> ministry is established; and they be these: Edinburgh, Saint
> Andrews, Dundee, Saint Johnston, Brechin, Montrose, Stirling,
> Ayr. And now, Christ Jesus is begun to be preached upon the
> south borders, next to you in Jedburgh and Kelso, also, so
> that the trumpet soundeth over all, blessed be our God.[1]

But not only among the Bible-reading merchants and their
wives in the City of London did Knox find eager friends and
disciples, but in the old Lollard stronghold along the Thames
Valley by the Chiltern hills. Among such, already ripe and ready
for something more austere and radical than was provided by
the one-step-forward-two-steps-back tactics of Cranmer and the
Bishops, Knox could speak freely as he did in his fateful discourse
at Amersham in which he likened Mary of England to Jezebel
and her uncle, Charles V to Nero—which no doubt roused an
admiring and consentient buzz at Amersham but which was to
procure his ignominious expulsion when read by Anglican laymen
to the Frankfurt magistrates a few years hence.

Knox's ministries in England and particularly in Berwick and
Newcastle had something of a Richard Baxter—Kidderminster—
flavour and they rightly procured his recognition by the government, his appointment as a royal Preacher and his offer of the

---

[1] Knox, *Works,* vi. 78.

bishopric of Rochester by Northumberland who thought of him as a goad to the more moderate episcopate.

It is among the company of Edwardian preachers that we see Knox in true proportion, alongside Latimer and Bradford, Coverdale and Hooper, Lever and Foxe. In two fine works, Pierre Janton has shown how the seemingly off-the-cuff extempore preaching of Latimer and Knox who rarely used manuscripts is really based on a fairly intricate reliance on the rules of rhetoric. Both were great popular preachers, deploying great resources of humour, irony and anecdote and veiled allusion. Both employed at the Court of Edward VI the brand of prophetic preaching, which like Zwingli's in Zürich and Calvin's in Geneva were able to bring scripture to bear on contemporary issues before an audience which included all who made the life of the community tick. Both named names and were specific in their denunciation of bribery and corruption: Knox with his devastating indictment of the Lord Treasurer in the guise of Shebna: Latimer again and again being charged with seditious speech for his naming of dignities. Though the phrase 'commonwealth men' has recently been under attack, Latimer and Lever and Knox were concerned with social justice and only too well aware of the dangers which lay in the rule of the hard faced men around Northumberland, or in Scotland, Mary, Queen of Scots. Then Knox has much in common with that other north of England preacher, John Bradford, whose letters from prison are the most important legacy of his career, and suggest him as the Dietrich Bonhoeffer of the Marian persecutions.

It was a sermon of Hugh Latimer which went like an arrow to the conscience of Bradford as a recently demobilised army officer, and which led him into holy orders as a late vocation, and a preacher whose theme moved always within the orbit of repentance. But in Bradford even more than in Lever or Latimer, there is this device of geographical expostulation—'O Manchester, repent. Turn to God O Bolton!'—which strikes the modern ear as grotesque to the point of comedy. But these Reformers were not nineteenth-century Evangelicals addressing individual sinners only. For them men stood under the Word as members of communities, in cities and in nations. This is the key to that prophetic hermeneutic so powerfully employed by Knox, which applied the Old Testament burdens of Israel almost univocally

to the political situation in their own day. One great example
of this is the massive three-hour discourse which he gave in St
Giles' in 1565 which mightily affronted the young Lord Darnley
on this, the only occasion when he ventured within range of
Knox's preaching. Moving and famous is the epilogue which
Knox penned, when weeks later he came to write it up.

> Lord! in thy hands I commend my spirit; for the terrible roaring
> of guns and the noise of armour, doth so pierce my heart, that
> my soul thirsteth to depart.[1]

But, no less than the castle of Edinburgh was the pulpit of
St Giles', 'Eyn, Feste Burg' which cracked and roared with
salvoes, no less effective than the cannon balls from the aptly
named gun nicknamed John Knox—with every quarter-of-an-
hour or so some magnificently insolent aside, always a scriptural
allusion, which took seconds to sink in, and the congregation
gasped. But behind it all there was a prophetic interpretation of
history. It was the historian Froude who said:

> One lesson and one only history may be said to repeat with
> distinctness, that in the long run it is well with the good, in
> the long run it is ill with the wicked . . . but this is simply the
> teaching of the Hebrew prophets.

Knox and John Foxe would have queried the words 'long run'
and we, remembering Auschwitz and Berlin, may wonder too
whether we have dismissed too easily the view that it is justice,
measured in divine terms, whereby empires rise and fall, and
without which, as Augustine saw, all power systems become
'robbers' caves'—the shattering truth that I belong to Glasgow,
but Glasgow belongs to God.

Both Knox and Bradford had correspondence with devout
ladies. This has little to do with sex. Knox's heart is revealed
in a dozen words to his own Marjory—'I think this be the first
letter I have written you'. Mother-in-law Bowes was no black
sheep, but a silly lamb, who supposed that the sins of Sodom and
Gomorrah were the things which came upon her daily as she
coped with bringing up a brood of children, and which she hung
round the neck of her son-in-law in a fantastic correspondence
in which her sins and anguishes were always out of date by the

[1] Knox, *Works*, vi. 273.

time he heard of them and turned aside from pressing business to comfort her. But this was a natural Protestant counterpart to the mediaeval confessional and to spiritual direction, and the new Protestant house groups or cells such as Knox directed in Scotland, Berwick, London, Geneva. The part played by godly women in them (as in the eighteenth century by ladies like Mary Bosanquet in the 'bands' of John Wesley) will only surprise those who forget that throughout Christian history women have always borne the greater share of the burden of Christian spirituality, their true, authentic ministry. But this bit of a letter from Bradford to Joyce Hales, who ministered to him and his friends in prison could have been penned by John Knox.

> If you were a market sheep you should do in more fat and grassy pasture. But because you are for God's own occupying therefore you must pasture on the bare common, abiding the storms and the tempest that fall . . . suffer a little and be still . . . for Christ is Emmanuel, God with us.

Both John Foxe and John Knox were historians and preachers and both gained a considerable reputation as seers: this not for any noticeably charismatic qualities but because their interpretation of history and their prophetic hermeneutic, in times of national religious crisis and decision, came true again and again, in Knox's case, when we have allowed for misreporting, tarradiddles of disciples and much hindsight, with a circumstantial quality which is startling and impressive.

In the latter part of his rather dreary treatise on predestination, Knox has an interesting digression about continental Anabaptists and he has an account of the decline and fall of Thomas Müntzer, the radical reformer of Saxony, who was a leader in the Thuringian sector of the Peasant War and was executed by the Princes after the catastrophe of Frankenhausen in the summer of 1525. Knox took his account from Sleidanus who lifted it from Melanchthon as it shows Müntzer as the Lutherans saw him, a fanatic incendiary. Knox would have been surprised, though perhaps Elizabeth would not, to know how much he had in common, superficially at least with the rebel leader. Both preachers had an apocalyptic sense of living in a time of judgment, and both Knox and Müntzer preached on the book of Daniel and appealed to Haggai. Both were learned men, without being academics and were preachers of great power, rabble-rousers indeed. Both preached Justification by Faith in Luther's terms but within a doctrine of the Church where predestination is central, with the true church as the little flock of the elect, menaced by the giant forces of the false church and of Antichrist. It was Müntzer who drew his followers into making Covenants, appealing first to the nobility—for Müntzer's famous sermon to the Princes shows that he would have gone along with them had they championed his cause, and then to the smaller gentry, the lairds—so that Müntzer's ally, Graf Gunther von Schwarzenberg, who was also the super-intendent of a Christian congregation, is a kind of Teutonic Erskine of Dun. Both Müntzer and Knox speak technically of 'judgments' (*Urteil*)—which were moral verdicts on what we might now call situation ethics, problems of conscience. Both claimed that in the oppression of an ungodly magistrate or a papist ruler, there was a duty and right of active resistance. Both became increasingly susceptible to the appeal to violence, and Müntzer's ugly 'all that crap about mercy' has its sad parallel in Knox's reference to 'foolish pity'. Both in the end merit the fine comment of Lord Eustace Percy:

> When once a man sets out to establish the Kingdom of God as an earthly polity, it matters little whether he defies the State or invokes its aid, whether the sword he plans to take is the rebel's or the king's. In either case, however much he may flatter himself that he has drawn the sword only as an emergency measure, he can never sheathe it again. Those who appeal to force for the limited uses of mere social order can limit their use of it—but not so the man who appeals to it as an instrument of perfection. The man who takes that sword is happy if he can perish by it; if he lives, he will be bound slave to it all his days.[1]

The period 1560–1660 which followed the establishment of the Reformation, the period of religious wars with their great non-theological content but with their frighteningly high motivation of zeal and bigotry and intolerance was to prove indeed what Paul Hasard calls a 'crisis of European conscience'. The possibility that the new age of Christian nations might have opened up a new kind of Christian world, with more diversity and freedom

[1] E. Percy, *John Knox*. London, 1935. 289.

and new opportunities for social justice and the expansion of human prosperity with the emergent science, was instead smothered in a revulsion against Christian truth, and Christian ways and Christian men. But it was not all loss. The Protestant Reformation and the Catholic revival which followed opened the way to better things with new forms of Christian proclamation and teaching, new forms of worship and of Christian discipline, new hopes for the commonalty of mankind. Eminent among the makers of these things was one with doughty mental fight and with matchless integrity, John Knox.

Knox the Man

Professor GORDON DONALDSON, Ph.D., D.Litt.

*Sir William Fraser Professor of Scottish History and
Palaeography, University of Edinburgh*

When people speak about 'John Knox' they all too often mean a
body of principles, a theory, a theology, and not infrequently the
principles which are labelled 'John Knox' may be principles which
Knox did not hold. Knox has been a kind of slogan; Knox has
been almost an abstraction, and in the slogan or the abstraction
the reality and the humanity of Knox have been lost sight of.

Yet Knox is the first figure, in all the centuries of Scottish
history down to his day, in whose case sufficient material exists to
furnish a rounded picture of an individual's personality. He is the
first Scot who left voluminous *Memoirs*—for that is what the
History of the Reformation really is—*Memoirs* which have survived
for our enlightenment. No previous generation can show anything to parallel it. Equally, he is the first Scot for whom we have
really personal correspondence in any bulk. Earlier private letters
occur only sporadically: nearly all the correspondence which has
survived from previous generations is official correspondence.
With Knox we have, almost for the first time in Scotland, a
quantity of intimate personal letters.

So Knox the man emerges, both in his own writings and in
those of others. Knox in the galleys, with a statue of the Blessed
Virgin thrust into his hands and 'advisedly looking about', as
he puts it,[1] before throwing it into the water. Knox writing to
his future wife and remarking, 'I *think* this be the first letter that
ever I wrote to you'.[2] Knox alluding, all too cryptically, in a letter
to his mother-in-law, to 'what I did standing in the cupboard
in Anwick', when, as he says, 'I thought that no creature had been
tempted as I was'.[3] Knox entertaining the Duke of Châtelherault
and the English ambassador to supper in his manse on the evening

---

[1] Knox, *History*, i. 108.   [2] Knox, *Works*, iii. 395.
[3] *Ibid.*, iii. 350.

of Advent Sunday 1562.[1] Knox on his deathbed, saying 'Go read where I cast my first anchor', the seventeenth chapter of St John.[2] In this particular glimpse the mind leaps forward two and a half centuries to the deathbed of Sir Walter Scott, when Lockhart read to him the fourteenth chapter of the same gospel.

The identification of Knox with principles, rather than the study of Knox as a human being, has resulted in a good deal of injustice, to the extent that Knox is apt to be saddled with a lot of actions and attitudes which were foreign to him. Not only so, but the identification of Knox with principles has, I believe, resulted sometimes in a failure to understand some episodes in his career. Historians and biographers have sought the explanation of Knox's actions and attitudes in the theories, the principles and the theology which are labelled 'John Knox', and have sometimes made a poor job of finding the explanation there. If, instead, the explanation is sought in simple human terms it can sometimes be found there. A great deal about Knox becomes clear if we once recognise that he acted not in the way that principles or abstractions would have dictated in an ideal world, but in the way that an ordinary human being, with all the strength and all the weakness of a human being, acted in a world of hard reality.

One of the problems about Knox which has intrigued me and which is the key to many of his actions is the question of his attitude to physical danger. To accuse Knox of timidity, still more of cowardice, seems almost *lèse-majesté*, and of course all the abstract principles and theories associated with him leave no room for such a simple human weakness as fear. Besides, after all, did not the Earl of Morton, as his valedictory remark over Knox's grave, say, 'Here lies one who neither feared not flattered any flesh'?[3] This appreciation by a contemporary is apt to be regarded as closing the subject. And yet I cannot see Knox's record as justifying Morton's eulogy. We should at least keep in mind the possibility that Knox may have been less of a lion than is often believed.

[1] *Selections from unpublished Manuscripts . . . illustrating the reign of Mary, Queen of Scotland. MDXLIII–MDLXVIII*, ed. J. Stevenson. Maitland Club, Glasgow, 1837. 106.

[2] *Memorials of Transactions in Scotland. A.D. MDLXIX–MDLXXIII by Richard Bannatyne*, ed. R. Pitcairn. Bannatyne Club, Edinburgh, 1836. 288.

[3] *The Autobiography and Diary of Mr James Melville*, ed. R. Pitcairn. Wodrow Society, Edinburgh, 1842. 60.

I see two passages in Knox's earlier life which may have had a lasting influence on him. One was his association with George Wishart. Knox, you remember, had carried a two-handed sword before Wishart for his protection. But, when Wishart was arrested, he advised Knox not to seek to join him in his martyrdom, saying, 'One is sufficient for a sacrifice'.[1] It rather recalls Our Lord's rebuke to Peter in the Garden of Gethsemane, when he bade him put up his sword. Wishart's advice, I suggest, may have implanted in Knox's mind the idea that he would be of more service alive than dead, and this was an idea which, I believe, influenced his later actions.

The other early episode which affected him was his experience in the galleys. The day-to-day hardships in the galleys may have been exaggerated. Although it seems that it was in the castle of Rouen, and not actually in the galleys, that Henry Balnaves, Knox's fellow-captive, was able to compose a treatise on justification, Knox was able to prepare a summary of it while he was actually on galley-service. Yet the regime in the galleys was based on an appeal to force and fear, and the overseer's lash must have been a constant threat. No ordinary man could undergo the experience without learning a dread of physical suffering, and also without coming to loathe and hate the system which it represented. If Knox was uncharitable to the French and to the prelates we have to remember this episode as some explanation. No one would look for a fair assessment of Hitler's regime from a man who had suffered in a Nazi concentration camp. As J. R. N. Macphail remarked long ago, 'Knox's experiences in the French galleys may not indeed have filled him with a spirit of sweet reasonableness'.[2]

The galley episode may also have been a lesson to Knox in another way as well. His presence in the galleys at all was the result of miscalculation. He had entered the castle of St Andrews in the expectation that the English would intervene to support Beaton's murderers and that together they would bring about a political and ecclesiastical revolution in which the reforming party would come into power in Scotland. It must have been to Knox's immense disgust that it was France and not England that intervened and that his own fate, owing to his miscalculation, was

[1] Knox, *History*, i. 69.
[2] *S.H.R.*, xxii. 19.

to be made a captive instead of emerging as a successful revolutionary. It would not be surprising if Knox took care never to
make such a miscalculation again.

Whether because of Wishart's precept or because of the lesson
of the galleys, Knox certainly showed what can best be called a
prudential regard for his own safety. When he was released from
the galleys he made for England, which under Edward VI was
at the time the safest place in Europe for zealous Protestants.
Before Edward died, however, Knox already had 'foresight of
trouble to come', for he knew that Edward would die and that
England under Mary Tudor would be no place for him. This was
why he refused an English bishopric. To people who have lost
sight of Knox the man and think of Knox as a complex of
principles and theories, his refusal of an English bishopric has
presented a problem. But in simple human terms there is no
problem. Knox said explicitly that he refused the bishopric
because of 'the foresight of trouble to come' and because he
realised that, as he said, the days would not be long that England
would give him bread.[1] His prudence may well have saved him
from the fate of some of those who were bishops under Edward—
Cranmer, Ridley, Latimer and Hooper. When Mary Tudor did
become queen of England, Knox lost little time in seeking elsewhere a security which he no longer had in England. His
conscience was uneasy, but he recalled that we should be innocent
as doves and wise as serpents, and interpreted this to mean that
he should imitate the dove, 'which can defend herself . . . only
by the witness of her wings.[2] He admitted that 'fleeing the country
declareth my fear'.[3] It was not for him to remain in the years of
persecution. Frankfort, and then Geneva, were more congenial.

He did visit Scotland, from September 1555 to July 1556, but
at a time when no one had been put to death for heresy for five
years and when the governor, Mary of Guise, and the primate,
John Hamilton, were vying with each other in leniency towards
the Protestants. At the sign of danger, he departed again, and the
circumstances were such that it was probably a relief to the
authorities as well as to him that all that took place was the
harmless demonstration of burning his effigy after he had left the
country.

Knox did not return to Scotland again until he was sure of

[1] Knox, *Works*, iii. 122.　　[2] *Ibid.*, iv. 223.　　[3] *Ibid.*, iv. 247.

support. In 1557 he came, a little reluctantly, as far as Dieppe, on the strength of a summons from some friends of the reformation, but when they realised that they had been over-optimistic they knew their man well enough to turn him back before he left France. Knox was in no hurry to repeat the experiment, and was rather more ready to contemplate a return *to England* after Elizabeth succeeded Mary Tudor in November 1558. He might possibly have settled permanently in England if Elizabeth had been willing to admit him. His arrival in Scotland in May 1559 was a calculated move, for the prospective opening of a revolt in that month had been advertised months before in the Beggars' Summons. Communications being what they were in those days, even in early summer, Knox cannot have known to a day when he would arrive, but his timing, if approximate, was good, and it was no accident that he landed at Leith on 2 May, ten days before the Beggars' Summons would become operative on 'Flitting Friday'.[1]

When the revolt began, it was not all plain sailing, and the fortunes of war wavered to and fro between the reforming party and the French troops of Mary of Guise. Thus Knox was accepted as minister of Edinburgh, but the regent returned to the area in force, and Knox then discreetly handed over his new charge to Willock, quite candidly on the ground that Edinburgh was 'dangerous'.[2] One cannot help feeling that Willock comes better out of this episode than does Knox. The next moment of danger was after the Riccio murder in March 1566. Knox almost certainly had foreknowledge, and he certainly approved, of the crime, but he again expected a revolution to follow it, as he had done after Beaton's murder at St Andrews in 1547. But this time, when the revolution did not take place, and the murderers were thwarted in their aim to take over the government, Knox hastily departed from Edinburgh for the safety of Ayrshire, which had been, he remarked, a 'receptacle of God's servants of old'.[3] He does not seem to have ventured to return to Edinburgh during all the troubled months which remained of Mary's personal reign, but went off instead on a private visit to England, partly to see how his sons were getting on at school there, and he was not back in his pulpit in St Giles' until a revolution had been finally accomplished and Mary had been captured at Carberry. Then, and only

---

[1] *S.H.R.*, xxxix. 175–6.   [2] Knox, *History*, i. 211.   [3] *Ibid.*, i. 48.

then, he came back in triumph, 'like a jackal moving in for the kill', as his latest biographer says.[1]

There was one more period of danger. When Mary's supporters, under Kirkcaldy of Grange, were holding Edinburgh Castle and from it commanding the town, Edinburgh was no place for Knox, so he took refuge in St Andrews, to return only shortly before his death.

Well, that is the record. Knox does not emerge as an heroic figure. He was never confronted, he never allowed himself to be confronted, as Cranmer and others had been, with the terrible alternatives of the stake or recantation. It may have been his knowledge that he would shrink if he were so confronted that led to his prudence. He has a revealing remark himself. When, after one of his interviews with Mary, 'some papists' remarked, 'He is not afraid', he replied, 'Why should the pleasing face of a gentlewoman effray me? I have looked in the faces of many angry men and yet have not been afraid *above measure*'.[2] That qualifying phrase, 'above measure', which, I repeat, is his own phrase, seems to me rather revealing. Among contemporary writings it reminds one of Sir James Melville's immortal qualifying phrase about Queen Mary's performance on the virginals: he said she played 'reasonably *for a queen*'.[3]

I am not accusing Knox of cowardice. I would go no further than to repeat what I said earlier, that he showed a prudential regard for his own safety. Professor Rupp said last night that Knox always marched towards the sound of the guns. But he liked to know which way the guns were firing. And why not? The Knox of popular imagination, the complex of principles and theology, the abstraction, could not of course be moved by such considerations. But Knox the man could be and was so moved. He was perhaps not by temperament of the stuff of which martyrs are made, but it was all plain common sense. He honestly believed that he was more use alive than dead and that while martyrs had their uses the reforming cause could not be left without leaders, of whom he counted himself one.

He counted himself one. That brings me to another aspect of

[1] J. Ridley, *John Knox*, Oxford, 1968. 465.

[2] Knox, *History*, ii. 46.

[3] *Memoirs of his own Life. By Sir James Melville of Halhill. MDXLIX–MDXCIII*, ed. T. Thomson. Bannatyne Club, Edinburgh, 1827. 124.

Knox the man, namely his conceit, his vanity, or, to put it more charitably and perhaps more accurately, his not unjustified confidence in his own ability. I have often remarked that, while Knox had many virtues, humility was not one of them. It is this lack of humility, this conceit, which colours the *History of the Reformation* and shapes Knox's place in Scottish historiography. It has often been pointed out that other contemporary sources have little or nothing to say of Knox. George Buchanan managed to tell the whole story of events in Scotland from the death of Mary of Guise in 1560 to the battle of Langside in 1568 without mentioning Knox except when he introduced him as the preacher at the coronation of James VI. Sir James Melville, in his *Memoirs*, which are, of course, as much coloured by Melville's self-importance as Knox's *History* is by his, does not mention Knox at all. The fact that contemporaries clearly did not take Knox at his own valuation must shed some doubt on some of his remarks. For example, there is the delightful tale of what happened when the reformers were in full retreat in Fife at the beginning of 1560. According to Knox, Mary of Guise exclaimed at that point, 'Where is now John Knox's God? My God is stronger than his, yea even in Fife'.[1] It is hard to believe this, in view of the fact that in all her quite voluminous correspondence Mary of Guise shows no sign of being aware of Knox's existence at all. The fact that Knox figures so large in all later accounts of the period arises from his authorship of his own *History of the Reformation*. One contemporary, you remember, said that Willock, not Knox, was primate of the reformers' religion:[2] but then Willock did not write a *History of the Reformation*.

I am not suggesting that Knox was unimportant. As minister of the capital he enjoyed a position of quite unique influence, his salary was, to put it in modern terms, not on the ministers' scale but on the superintendents' scale, in the Register of Ministers and their Stipends his name appears in glorious isolation, set apart from ministers and superintendents alike, he was made much off by the town council of Edinburgh, he hobnobbed with notables of all kinds, including royalty. It is in these facts that we have the explanation, again in simple human terms, of Knox's

[1] Knox, *History*, i. 277.
[2] *The Miscellany of the Wodrow Society*, ed. D. Laing. Wodrow Society, Edinburgh, 1844, i. 267.

refusal of a superintendentship, which some have found as puzzling as his earlier refusal of a bishopric. When he said, in declining a superintendentship, that he thought his estate 'honourable enough',[1] he was not suggesting that he thought the honour of being an ordinary parish minister was all he wanted: he meant exactly what he said—his estate as minister of the capital was honourable enough for the most ambitious man. He also said, less convincingly, that instead of being a bishop, he would rather be 'a painful preacher of the blessed evangel',[2] but this was convention. I can well imagine Knox saying, 'I'd much rather be an ordinary minister', but he knew, and everyone else knew, that he was not an ordinary minister. He can hardly have failed to see which side his bread was buttered on. If he did not, perhaps his wife did. Mrs Knox—the first Mrs Knox—died in December 1560, but it is possible that by that time Knox had already refused a superintendentship. And it is not difficult to think of Marjory putting her point of view: 'No, indeed, John, you're not going to leave your comfortable Edinburgh manse, where you have a wealthy and distinguished congregation within easy reach, and go gadding round the country, wearing yourself out and catching chills, to do the work of a superintendent, and in the end get neither more money nor more thanks for it all'. And the uxorious Knox gave way. This imaginary scene reminds me of a minister of a poor and remote country parish who was, quite unexpectedly, offered a call to a wealthy city charge. A friend of the family came to the manse door to be met by the minister's daughter. He asked her what news there was about her father's decision. 'Well,' she said, 'Daddy's in the study praying for guidance, and Mummy's upstairs packing.' Knox's attitude is perfectly clear in simple human terms, but people find it hard to accept because they refuse to think of him in simple human terms and look for explanations in the subtleties of opinions on ecclesiastical polity. J. D. Mackie, for instance, protested that the argument that Knox was too comfortable as a minister of Edinburgh was hardly a good argument.[3] He could not bring himself to believe that Knox acted like a sensible human being.

[1] *Cal. S.P. Scot.*, i. No. 967.
[2] Knox, *Works*, vi. 559: cf. *Cal. S.P. Scot.*, iv. No. 452.
[3] J. D. Mackie, *John Knox*. London, 1951. 17.

Knox unquestionably has his real importance in the Scotland of his day. But I still think there was an element of vanity in the man, exceeding what his position entitled him to possess. And a man of his vanity, his self-importance, could, I suggest, easily suffer from wounded pride, which from time to time affected his attitude and his actions. For example, he suffered humiliation at the hands of the so-called 'Anglican' party at Frankfort, and I believe this did something to colour his attitude to some men in the Church of England from whom he was not in truth separated by any very profound differences on either polity or liturgy. He was humiliated again when he took the trouble to write a long epistle to Mary of Guise which she handed to one of her courtiers with the remark, 'Please you, my lord, to read a pasquil'. Mary became the object of his unrelenting hatred. And he was humiliated yet once more when he was refused permission to enter England in 1559. There had never been any hope of an accommodation with Elizabeth after he had written the First Blast of his Trumpet, but England's refusal to accept him in 1559 was something which he probably never forgave. It was not a humble man who wrote indignantly, 'England in refusing me refuseth a friend'.[1] His furious anger at this point found expression not only in a letter to Cecil but in a swinging and extravagant attack on the Prayer Book, written a few days later, to which I shall return.

Knox's human nature also, I suggest, explains his occasional inconsistencies. One obvious example of inconsistency is Knox's varying judgment of the question of where the best reformed church was to be found. In December 1556 he wrote that Geneva was 'the most perfect school of Christ that ever was in earth since the days of the Apostles' and in April 1559 he described Geneva as 'the most godly reformed church and city of the world'.[2] But by 1566, by which date he had got a reformed church organised in Scotland, he did not think so favourably of Geneva: 'As touching the doctrine taught by our ministers, and as touching the administration of sacraments used in our churches, we are bold to affirm that there is no realm this day upon the face of the earth that hath them in greater purity; yea (we must speak the truth whomsoever we offend), there is none (no realm, we mean) that hath them in the like purity. For all others (how sincere that ever the doctrine be, that by some is taught) retain in their

[1] Knox, *History*, i. 286–7.   [2] Knox, *Works*, iv. 240, 283.

churches and the ministers thereof, some footsteps of Antichrist, and some dregs of papistry; but we (all praise to God alone) have nothing within our churches that ever flowed from that Man of Sin'.[1] If there is inconsistency here, which shows Knox's human nature, there may be another element which likewise shows it: Knox, in spite of all his imitation of England and his adulation of Geneva, was a good Scot, a good enough Scot to cry, 'Here's tae us, wha's like us?' It is not in the nature of theories and principles to be inconsistent, but it is very human to be inconsistent. There may have been not only inconsistency; there may have been unresolved tensions in Knox's own mind. For example, in one of his interviews with Mary there was a celebrated retort. When the Queen asked, 'What have you to do with my marriage, or what are you within this commonwealth', Knox replied, 'A subject born within the same, Madam. And albeit I neither be Earl, Lord nor Baron within it, yet has God made me (how abject that ever I be in your eyes) a profitable member within the same'.[2] This does reflect Knox's vanity, but in this answer, it has been said with pardonable exaggeration, 'modern democracy was born'.[3] Yet the man who thus expressed modern democracy was also the man who expressed, more clearly than any other, the traditional Scottish bonds of kinship and service, which were assuredly mediaeval and not modern. He admitted to the Earl of Bothwell: 'I have borne a good mind to your house: and have been sorry at my heart of the troubles that I have heard you be involved in. For, my Lord, my great-grandfather, grandfather and father have served your Lordship's predecessors, and some of them have died under their standards; and this is a part of the obligation of our Scottish kindness'.[4] A remark perhaps paralleled only by that of a Borderer who said that if his chief would turn him out at the front door he would come in again at the back door.[5]

Again, I think there may all along have been an unresolved tension between warm-hearted evangelicalism and hard-headed

[1] Knox, *History*, ii. 3.
[2] *Ibid.*, ii. 83.
[3] *Ibid.*, ii. 83 n. 1.
[4] *Ibid.*, ii. 38.
[5] David Hume of Godscroft, *History of the House of Douglas and Angus*. Edinburgh, 1743, ii. 260.

common sense or realism. Yet again, there was the inconsistency between human warmth on one hand and perhaps equally human hatred on the other. Once more we turn to one of the interviews with Mary. When Knox reduced her to tears, he protested: 'I never delighted in the weeping of any of God's creatures; yea, I can scarcely well abide the tears of my own boys whom my own hand corrects, much less can I rejoice in your Majesty's weeping'.[1] Yet this same man, who protested that he never delighted in the sufferings of any of God's creatures, was able to express delight in the sufferings of God's creatures when they happened to be in a different camp from himself, like Francis II and Mary of Guise. Francis, he rejoiced, perished of 'a rotten ear, . . . that deaf ear that never would hear the truth of God'.[2] Before Mary's death, then 'began her belly and loathsome legs to swell'.[3] In these remarks, said Professor Dickinson, 'there is a narrow hate that diminishes the stature of the man and that chills us as we read.'[4]

Then there is the question of Knox's relations with women. I see human nature rather than principle here. It is true that some of the reformers did marry purely as a matter of principle, to show their disapproval of celibacy. But I do not think this explains Knox. He had, to begin with, remarkable tenderness for females, as his correspondence amply shows, and he established a number of very intimate friendships. It was a curious relationship in most cases, not at all a sexual relationship in the ordinary sense and yet, as has been acutely remarked—and remarked by a woman—it was a relationship which could have existed only between persons of different sexes. It must be remembered that all those women who wrote to Knox, talked to Knox and very often wept with Knox, were women who had been accustomed to auricular confession under the old system and, if they had been fortunate in their confessors, may have been accustomed to pouring out their hearts to a man. Knox may well have been a peculiarly sensitive, sympathetic and understanding father confessor who did not think those women at all tiresome, as a different man might have done. 'Here was this great-voiced, bearded man of God, who might be seen beating the solid pulpit every Sunday, and who on the Monday would sit in their parlours by the hour, and weep with them over their manifold trials and

[1] Knox, *History*, ii. 83.   [2] *Ibid.*, i. 347, 349.
[3] *Ibid.*, i. 319.   [4] *Ibid.*, i. lxxiii.

temptations. Nowadays, he would have to drink a dish of tea with all these penitents.'.[1]

Reverting to the question of marriage as a matter of principle, I doubt if anyone would allege that Knox's second marriage, in 1564, when he was at least fifty, probably more, and the bride was a girl of seventeen, was contracted as a matter of principle. It is, however, fair to observe that Knox had, at the time of that second marriage, been a widower for nearly four years. I see no reason to think him a man who was strongly moved by sexual passion, and the scurrilous tales about his ongoings which his enemies put about are so completely out of character as to be discounted. Knox's first marriage is illuminating. He may or may not have been deeply in love with Marjory Bowes, but a man of strong sexual passion would hardly have set up that extraordinary triangular household which contained both Marjory and her mother. Knox was the kind of man who would have taken his mother-in-law on his honeymoon. The fact is that Mrs Bowes really did desert her husband to keep in Knox's company, and Knox was certainly open to the charge of enticement. His in-laws, the Bowes family, had probably never been very keen on even his marriage to Marjory, and the later friction with them and especially with the grass-widower Sir Robert, adds a peculiarly human dimension to Knox.

It would certainly not be an over-statement to say that Knox was not indifferent to women or to say that in his own way he was also attractive to women. I wonder if this very human side of Knox may throw some light on his relations with Mary, Queen of Scots. It is admitted on all sides that Mary was a charmer, not indeed because of striking beauty but because of her fine skin, her carriage and her vivacious personality. Englishmen, who were not her subjects, were sufficiently impressed. One remarked that 'She hath withal an alluring grace, a pretty Scotch accent, and a searching wit, clouded with mildness'.[2] Another, who was a conscientious Puritan and might have been expected to be as hostile as Knox, declared Mary 'a notable woman' and said he must commend her 'ready wit and constant courage', and he burst out 'What is to be done with such a lady and princess, or whether

[1] R. L. Stevenson, 'John Knox and his Relations with Women', in *Familiar Studies of Men and Books*. London, 1882. 395.
[2] A. Fraser, *Mary, Queen of Scots*. London, 1969. 415.

such a puissant lady is to be nourished in one's bosom, or whether
it be good to halt and dissemble with such a lady, I refer to your
judgment'.[1]

How different to turn to Knox's words: 'If there be not in her
a proud mind, a crafty wit and an indurate heart against God and
His truth, my judgment faileth me'.[2] Are we to believe that Knox
alone was unmoved, or that Knox saw further and deeper than
any of his contemporaries? I find it easier to believe that Knox
was not in fact indifferent to Mary's charms and that all his
expressed hostility arose from the need he felt to build up a
deliberate and conscious resistance lest he should give way to the
emotions which his heart dictated.

If Knox was less austere towards women than is apt to be
believed, he was less austere to other things as well. He is
habitually blamed for an excessive puritanism—here is the slogan
coming in again—an excessive puritanism which was, I think,
really foreign to his nature. Puritanism there was, but it was a
puritanism which prevailed widely at the time and was not the
monopoly of Knox and the Protestants. As I see it, a necessary
and desirable reaction against the grossly relaxed discipline of
late mediaeval times produced a strong puritanical strain which
manifested itself in many ways and in many places. For example,
the Catechism put out in Scotland by Archbishop John Hamilton
in 1552 was forceful on the subject of Sunday observance and
roundly condemned dancing as an incitement to lechery. Knox
was in fact more moderate, because in his day public houses were
open on Sunday (except in time of sermon). It was only after his
death that penalties were imposed for both working and playing
on Sundays, and in one of his interviews with Queen Mary he
told her that he did not utterly condemn dancing. Somewhat
similarly, it was not the reformers, but the Catholic administration
of Queen Mary's mother, that first tried to suppress the traditional
May Day festivities associated with Robin Hood and Little John,
which were held to lead to much unseemly conduct. To take
another illustration, and going further afield for the parallel, it is
true that in Knox's time the Edinburgh town council issued a
proclamation banishing all harlots from the town, but it is also
true that Pius V, a Counter-Reformation pope who died in the
same year as Knox, issued an edict expelling the prostitutes from

[1] *Cal. S.P. Scot.*, ii. Nos. 678, 679, 768.   [2] Knox, *History*, ii. 20.

Rome. The Pope was so fastidious that he insisted on covering up the nakedness of classical statues. In the Scotland of Knox, by contrast, homes were decorated with painted ceilings which are sometimes improper if not obscene. Besides, literary works like those of Sir David Lindsay, containing as they do much ribaldry, were twice reprinted in Knox's years of ministry at St Giles'. One printer of Knox's time even inserted a 'bawdy song' in his edition of the metrical psalter, though admittedly he was censured by the General Assembly.

I am sure that Knox was human enough to join in the general gaiety. Perhaps he would have agreed with the Rector of Old St Paul's Church, who declared recently that the best answer to the current wave of pornography is what he called 'holy laughter'. He certainly had a strong sense of humour, which comes out repeatedly in his history. He liked a joke—and a broad joke at that. But his humour comes out at its best in some of his passages of narrative.

Both his humour and his human nature come out, again, in his occasional exaggerations and extravagances of expression. He was apt to say more than he meant, and sometimes was quite deliberately trailing his coat. An outstanding example is his letter to Mrs Locke in April 1559 about the Prayer Book. 'One jot', he roundly declared, 'of these diabolical inventions, viz. crossing in Baptism, kneeling at the Lord's Table, mummelling or singing of the Litany, *a fulgure et tempestate, a subitanea et improvisa morte* etc., will I never counsel any man to use'.[1] His use of Latin phraseology when he purports to be criticising an English litany itself suggests extravagance, and his awareness that he was putting an exaggerated point of view emerges when he says to his correspondent, 'I appear to jest with you'.

In this matter again, as I have pointed out, there was inconsistency. Although he had said so plainly that he would never counsel any man to use the diabolical inventions of the Prayer Book, yet when English Puritans came to him, telling him that their consciences dictated that they must leave the Church of England, he told them to go back home and conform, and in effect use these same diabolical inventions.[2] In other words, we

[1] Knox, *Works*, vi. 12.
[2] G. Donaldson, *The Making of the Scottish Prayer Book of 1637*. Edinburgh, 1954. 11.

must not take everything Knox said as literal truth. He was rather big-mouthed and loud-mouthed, and liked to exaggerate to emphasise or over-emphasise a point.

Another example of his extravagance and exaggeration of language is his remark that he feared one Mass more than if 10,000 armed men were landed in the realm to suppress the whole religion.[1] But two years before, all his arguments had been based on the presence in Scotland of not 10,000, but only about 4000, French troops and not on the saying of Mass when Mass was being said not once but hundreds of times.

Now, all this extravagance of language is a very human trait. We must remember that some of the quotations come from private letters, which were surely not intended to be read four centuries after they were written and by persons other than the recipient. And who does not let himself go occasionally in a private letter in a way he would not let himself go in a public statement or in print? Even his *History* may have been written for a limited readership who would share the author's prejudices or who would know him well enough to understand when he was exaggerating.

At any rate, I certainly do not take as literal truth a good many of Knox's own statements as he reports them in his *History*. We all know the kind of man who likes to say, 'And I just said to him . . .', or, 'And I just told him . . .', and we know very well that very often he has said no such thing. I remember one individual of this type, much given to noisy assertions about what he had said or what he was going to say, and he once caught himself up. He said that day, 'And I just said—I mean I might have said'. We might perhaps keep this kind of thing in mind when we try to compose a rounded, complete picture of the complexities of strength and weakness, warmth and hatred, haste and calculation, exaggeration and caution, which all go to make up Knox the Man.

[1] Knox, *History*, ii. 12.

Knox the Writer

DAVID D. MURISON, M.A., B.A.

Editor, Scottish National Dictionary, and
Honorary Senior Lecturer, University of Edinburgh

Enough has already been said about Knox to show the difficulty of portraying such a contradictory and complex character, at once so mercurial and devious and yet so unflinchingly or, according to your sympathies, so appallingly single-minded. The same applies equally to Knox the writer, none the less in that Knox never claimed to be a literary man at all. In the preface to his one published sermon he says 'Wonder not . . . that of al my studye and travayle within the Scriptures of God these twentye yeares, I have set forth nothing in exponing anye portion of Scripture . . . considering my selfe rather cald of my God to instruct the ignorant, comfort the sorrowfull, confirme the weake, and rebuke the proud, by tong and livelye voyce, in these corrupt dayes, than to compose bokes for the age to come.'[1] In his own eyes he was essentially a propagandist, God's mouthpiece, a trumpet, as he repeatedly called himself; most of his writings are the unpremeditated product of the needs or feelings of the moment, frequently dashed off under stress, formless and repetitive in great part, as most propaganda is, and yet one at least of his works can still hold our interest and attention after four hundred years.

They follow closely the circumstances of his life, and Knox the writer is inextricably mixed up with Knox the man, but there is a kind of pattern visible in both and it can be divided roughly into four parts or aspects; of Knox the pastor in his letters to various friends, comrades and members of his congregations; Knox the theologian in his treatises on prayer, on predestination, and in his disputations with Roman Catholic spokesmen; Knox the pamphleteer in his various public letters, admonitions and blasts of the trumpet, to adopt the key words in their titles; and finally Knox the historian and apologist *pro vita sua*.

[1] Knox, *Works*, vi. 229.

His first work, written in 1548 while he was still a galley slave, was addressed to the Congregation who had been with him in St Andrews and were now in fact his fellow-prisoners in France and much in need of the encouragement and optimism of the letter. Whatever their present misfortunes and apparent defeat, Knox assured them that if they only adhered to God's word and commandment, having once seen the light, they were bound to triumph—and plenty of Scriptural parallels are adduced to prove this—whereas the ungodly, the Roman Catholics of course, who preferred to remain in darkness, were equally certain to come ultimately to disaster. This was Knox's basic position throughout his life. It was the faith that moved mountains. And while of course any devout Christian might argue thus in general *a priori* from God's omnipotence and grace, Knox does attempt to carry conviction by arrogating to himself a kind of prophetic gift which I suspect was part of the secret of the success of his preaching. One can hardly speak of second sight in this connection and he expressly repudiates any supernatural pretensions, though the Roman Catholics said bluntly that he was a warlock—'My assurances are not the Mervallis of Merlin, nor yit the dark sentences of prophane Prophesies; But . . . the plane treuth of Godis Word'.[1] But yet 'I dare not denye (lest that in so doing I should be injurious to the giver) but that God hath revealed unto me secretes unknown to the worlde'.[2] So he hedges somewhat in introducing a little mystification in support of his prophecies.

Knox was in any case obsessed by the logic of God in history, and I use the word 'logic' advisedly, because Knox's mental training was mediaeval and Aristotelian. If it is true that he studied under John Major at St Andrews,[3] then he heard the last of the Scottish scholastics, and according to Beza rivalled his master in metaphysics. One might indeed say that he was brought up on the syllogism.

This comes out in his discourse at Newcastle in 1550 in defending his condemnation of the Mass. 'All worshipping, honoring or service inventit by the braine of man in the religioun of God,

[1] Knox, *Works*, iii. 168.

[2] *Ibid.*, vi. 229.

[3] According to Beza: Glasgow according to others. Cf. J. Ridley, *John Knox*. Oxford, 1968, 15–17 with footnotes and Appendix II. This view is disputed by J. K. Cameron in *S.H.R.*, xlviii. 185.

without his express commandment, is Idolatrie; the Masse is inventit be the braine of man, without any commandement of God: Thairfoir it is Idolatrie.'[1] This was the type of proposition in which all Knox's thinking is couched—all resting of course on the antecedent premiss which he expresses thus: 'In religioun thair is na middis: either it is the religioun of God, and that in everie thing that is done it must have the assurance of his awn Word, and than is his Majestie trewlie honourit, or els it is the religioun of the Divill, whilk is, when men will erect and set up to God sic religioun as pleaseth thame; and no dout is the Divill honourit.'[2]

Granting this hypothesis and the rigorous logic with which it is developed and brushing aside the awkward question of who is to interpret God's word, Knox is on pretty unshakable ground, and it was the boundless confidence it produced that made Knox so ready to challenge his opponents to debate, from university lecturers to the Queen herself. It is noteworthy that his two most formidable antagonists, Kennedy and Winget, avoided direct confrontation on the Scriptural issue and tried to get at Knox on different grounds altogether. Knox in fact was using against the old Church the very weapon it had forged for itself over the centuries—the logic of the schools.

There is besides in the Newcastle sermon much skilful rhetoric, long Ciceronian periods interspersed with direct questions to the Catholics: 'By whome haif thai that name, I desyre to know? By Jesus Chryst, will thai say? . . . will ye then say, that the Congregatioun of the Corinthians wer Papist preistis? . . . But, O Papistis! is God a juglar? Useth he certane nomber of wordis in performing his intent?'[3]

There is some sarcasm but the language is temperate and restrained and the general impression is of one in solid and assured control of his argument.

In the next three years Knox, now in England, found himself more deeply and not altogether unwillingly involved in the high politics of Edward VI's reign as a preacher of outspoken sermons pushing the Reformation further to the left. But with the death of Edward and the accession of Mary, Protestantism and Knox himself were in serious danger; and here we come to another aspect of the man.

[1] Knox, *op. cit.*, iii. 34.　　[2] *Ibid.*, iv. 232.　　[3] *Ibid.*, iii. 50–51.

He knew what this would mean for the small scattered groups of Protestants throughout England and as with the Congregation of St Andrews he had to comfort them as best he could. It is true that he himself fled to the Continent, an action which troubled his conscience later not a little as we shall see. Not unnaturally as a Christian, he directed them to prayer, and left behind a short treatise for surreptitious publication with the fictitious and typically sardonic Knoxian imprint: 'At Rome before the Castel of St Aungel at the signe of St Peter'.[1] It was described as 'A declaratioun what trew Prayer is, how we suld Pray, and for what we suld Pray'.[2]

It is one of Knox's most attractive works showing him at his best in pastoral theology. It is written in a simple direct style, well reasoned as always, with plenty of Scriptual 'proofs', as we call them in Scotland: his definition of prayer seems unexceptionable to all believers: 'Prayer is ane earnest and familiar talking with God, to whome we declair oure miseries, whois support and help we implore and desyre in our adversiteis, and whome we laude and prais for oure benefittis receaved';[3] though there are indirect criticisms of Catholic practices, he avoids polemics and his tone is mild, gentle and persuasive, all the more so in that here and there he lifts the veil from his own inner life and talks as one who has known suffering, despair and spiritual tension himself. The worst he had to say against the intercession of saints was again by rhetorical question: 'Is he who discendit from heaven, and vouchsaffit to be conversant with synneris, commanding all soir vexit and seik to cum unto him, (who, hanging upon the Cross, prayit first for his ennemyis) becum now so untractable, that he will not heir us without a persone to be a meane [intermediary]? O Lord! oppin the eis of suche, that thai may cleirlie persave thy infinit kyndnes, gentilnes and love toward mankynd';[4] and of the need to obey God rather than man he says: 'the fraill flesche, oppressit with feir and pane, desyreth delyverance, ever abhoring and drawing back frome obedience giving. O Christiane Brethrene, I wryt be experience: but the Spreit of God calleth back the mynd to obedience, that albeit it doith desyre and abyd for delyverance, yit suld it not repyne aganis the gudwill of God, but incessantlie ask that it may abyde with pacience: How hard

---

[1] Knox, *op. cit.,* iii. 81. [2] *Ibid.,* iii. 83.
[3] *Ibid.* [4] *Ibid.,* iii. 98.

this battell is, no man knawith but he whilk in himself hath
sufferit tryell.[1]. . . I knaw the grudgeing and murmuring com-
playntes of the flesche; I knaw the angir, wraith, and indignatioun
whilk it consavith aganis God, calling all his promissis in doubt,
and being reddie everie hour utterlie to fall frome God. Aganis
whilk restis onlie faith.'[2]

But we see even deeper into Knox's character in a collection
of letters to various ladies who had been members of his congregations, above all his own mother-in-law, Elisabeth Bowes.
His letters to Mrs Bowes, who appears to have suffered from
religious melancholia, reveal not a little of Knox's own spiritual
state, in trying to advise and comfort her. He has obviously
been through all the battles of temptation and failure and mortifi-
cation himself, but has also found hope of salvation and in a
patient and gentle manner does his best to pass this on to her.

'Sister, remember that the power, myght, and vertew of Jesus
oure Savioure is maid knawn in oure weaknes. He dispyssis not
the lame and krukit scheip; na, he tackis the same upon his back
and bearis it to the flock becaus it may not ga; that sa the un-
speakable mercie and kyndnes of the Scheiphird may be knawn
and praisit of us his scheip. War we alwayis strang, than suld we
not taist how sweit and mercifull the releif of oure God is fra theis
daylie cairis; and sa suld we grow proude, negligent and unmynd-
full, whilk estait is maist dangerous of all uthiris.'[3]

It was to these ladies that Knox reveals himself in his intro-
spective moods which, as one might expect from a Calvinist,
were frequent enough. He frankly faces the dilemma of every
sincere and thoughtful preacher: 'Albeit I never lack the presence
and plane image of my awn wreachit infirmitie, yit seing syn sa
manifestlie abound in al estaitis, I am compellit to thounder out
the threattnyngis of God aganis obstinat rebellaris; in doing
whairof . . . I sumtymes am woundit, knawing my self criminall
and giltie in many, yea in all . . . thingis that in utheris I reprehend.'[4]

He is human enough to long for true friends: 'Of nature I am
churlish, and in conditions different from many; Yet one thing
I ashame not to affirme, that familiaritie once throughlie contracted was never yet brocken on my default' (and we know later
on from the *History* how deeply he felt his estrangement from

---

[1] Knox, *op. cit.*, iii. 100. [2] *Ibid.*, iii. 101–2.
[3] *Ibid.*, iii. 339. [4] *Ibid.*, iii. 338.

the Regent Moray and from Kirkcaldy of Grange), and he adds
with humility: 'The cause may be that I have rather need of all
then that any hath need of me'.[1]

Again we see the struggles of conscience in his letter from
Geneva to two Protestant ladies in Edinburgh expressing concern
about his departure and prolonged absence from Scotland when
he thought the Queen Regent was about to step up the persecution of the Reformers. 'The cause of my stop I do not to this
day clearlie understand',[2] and he prays that his apparent timidity
and indecision may be 'na sclander to that doctrine whilk I
profess'.[3] His letters to Mrs Bowes are similarly full of misgivings
about his own conduct in fleeing from England. Whatever we
think of Knox in this, we must at least recognise the fact and the
frankness of a man in an agonising reappraisal of himself.

In a lighter vein we have Knox called in by the Edinburgh
ladies to adjudicate on how they should dress and writing gravely:
'It is verie difficill and dangerous to apoynt any certantie, leist in
sa doing we either restrane Christiane libertie, or else loose the
brydill too far to the folische fantassie of facil flesche'.[4] Notice
the old literary tradition of alliteration in this masterpiece of tact
and diplomacy or, if you like, wiliness, a quality which was to
stand Knox in good stead later in many a weightier matter.
Occasionally also we get a foretaste of that sarcastic humour which
permeates the *History*. He tells Mrs Locke of his activities in
St Andrews in achieving reformation there and how the Archbishop threatened that if he attempted to preach, 'twelve hacque-
butts sould light upoun my nose at once', adding his own
comment: '(O burning charitie of a bloodie bishop!)'[5] There is
plenty more of that to come.

Of course he was not always tactful and diplomatic. When he
felt he had to thunder, which was to be sure very frequently, he
thundered to some tune. Writing to Cecil for a permit to travel
through England from Dieppe to Scotland, he addressed the
English Secretary of State as follows: 'To the suppression of
Christ's true Evangell, to the erectinge of Idolatry, and to the
sheddinge of the bloode of God's deare children have you, by
silence, consented and subscribed. This your horrible defection

---

[1] Knox, *op. cit.*, vi. 11.   [2] *Ibid.*, iv. 250.
[3] *Ibid.*, iv. 253.   [4] *Ibid.*, iv. 225–6.
[5] *Ibid.*, vi. 25.

from the trueth knowne and professed, hathe God unto this day
mercifully spared. . . . Very love compelleth me to say, that
[except] the Spirit of God purge your hart from that venyme, . . .
that you shall not longe escape the rewarde of dissemblers'.[1] It
is difficult to imagine the present Archbishop of Canterbury
addressing the Foreign Secretary in such terms. Nor is it surprising
that Knox did not get his permit.

In his exile abroad he had time to work out his political theories
in a series of writings mostly addressed to the Protestants in
England, two *Comfortable Epistles, A Letter to the Faithful,* and
a *Faithful Admonition.* Here we have Knox as the political
pamphleteer. His arguments are well arranged and though he
disclaims oratorical skill, they are all in fact further examples of
lively rhetorical appeals: 'O, deare Brethrene, remember the
dignitie of oure vocatioun; you haif followit Christ: you haif
proclamit warre against ydolatrie; you haif laid hand upon the
treuth, and hes communicate with the Lordis tabill: Will ye now
suddanelie slyde back? Will ye refuse Christ and his truth, and
mak pactioun with the Devill and his dicevable doctrine? Will
ye tread the maist precious blude of Chrystis Testament under
your feit, and set up an idoll befoir the people?'[2]

It is in the *Admonition* however that the popular picture of
Knox as a master of invective begins to present itself. He lets
himself go, in alliterative denunciation of the pro-Catholic
bishops, 'poysoned Papistes', 'wyly Winchester, dreaming
Duresme and bloudy Bonner, with the rest of their bloudy
butcherly brood'.[3] As for 'mischievous Mary, that Jezebell!' 'Doth
she not manifestlye shewe her selfe to be an open traitoresse of
the Imperiall Crown of England, contrary to the juste lawes of
the Realme, to brynge in a straunger, and make a proude
Spaniarde kynge, to the shame, dishonoure, and destruction of the
nobilitie; . . . to the abasyng of the yeomanry, to the slavery of
the communaltie, to the overthrowe of Christianitie and Goddes
true religion?'[4] Knox's reference to a foreign King was a very
astute appeal to English nationalism, fully justified by the sequel;
and he was learning four centuries before the political expertise
of our own age the basic technique of propaganda—the constant
repetition of key ideas and words, *idolatry, corruption, error,*

[1] Knox, *op. cit.,* vi. 16–17.   [2] *Ibid.,* iii. 210.
[3] *Ibid.,* ii. 284–5.   [4] *Ibid.,* iii. 295.

damnation, murderers, bloody men, abomination, filthy, diabolical enemies of truth, pestilent Papist, superstition and so on.

During his brief stay in Scotland in 1555–56 he apparently at first imagined that he could really talk the Queen Regent, who was a Guise, into support of the Reformation and he addressed an open letter to her which begins in a striking declamatory way: 'The eternall providence of the ever-lyvynge God hath appointed his chosen children to fight in this wretched and transitory lyfe, a battel difficil, and the maner of their preservation in the same battel to be more mervellous. Their victory standeth not in resisting, but in suffering. And how they can be preserved, and not brought to uttermoste confusion, the eye of man perceyveth not.'[1]

This again is the sign of a skilled rhetorician, by cleverly stating a paradox at the outset to engage the reader's interest in its solution. The letter itself is firm and there is no mincing of words but its terms are courteous and dignified and even conciliatory. The Queen ignored it but described it as a pasquil or lampoon, a jibe for which Knox never forgave her and later, in his *History*, replied to in kind. Two years later he was to fall foul of other royal ladies in a much more resounding manner in the pamphlet with the forever memorable title of *The First Blast of the Trumpet against the Monstruous Regiment of Women*, basically an appeal to the people of England to rebel against their Queen.

Knox had been working his way to this theory for some years and had taken up a more advanced position than Calvin and the Zwinglians. Some of it turns up in the profuse notes to the Geneva translation of the Bible of 1560 in which Knox may well have had some hand and which became the standard version for Scotland after the Reformation, the chief cause incidentally of the progressive anglicisation of the old Scots language.[2]

---

[1] Knox, *op. cit.,* iv, 75.

[2] Cf. Ridley, *Knox.* 288–90. Knox himself seems to have been completely bilingual in Scots and English. The language of his works varies from pure English, as in his treatises on prayer and predestination, in *The First Blast* and in his public letters to the English Protestants, to a Scots-English mixed in differing degrees in his private letters and in his *History*. His style becomes more noticeably Scottish on his return to Scotland, but he never writes pure Scots. We do not always know how much is due to various secretaries, copyists and printers through whom most of his extant writings have been transmitted. His Roman Catholic antagonists taunted him with anglicising

Politics apart, *The First Blast* as literature cannot be said to rank high. Knox appears in it as a mediaevalist and a schoolman, in which he formulates at the outset the propositions to be proved, 'To promote a Woman to beare rule, superioritie and dominion, or empire above any Realme, Nation, or Citie, is repugnant to Nature; contumelie to God, a thing most contrarious to his reveled will and approved ordinance; and finallie, it is the subversion of good Order, of all equitie and justice.'[1] And he goes on in syllogisms to prove his points showing not inconsiderable learning in quoting from Aristotle, the Roman jurists, Saint Paul and the Church Fathers, Tertullian, Ambrose, Augustine, Chrysostom, the Fathers especially in support of anti-feminism. As is usual with so much scholastic argument it is dull, involved and repetitive. But at times the rhetorician takes over and livens things up, for instance, in wild exaggeration—'This monstriferouse empire of Women (which amongest all enormities that this day do abound upon the face of the whole earth, is most detestable and damnable).'[2] His first argument gets side-tracked by passionate denunciations of Mary and her government, and he finally has to pull himself up saying—'Albeit I have thus (talkinge with my God in the anguishe of my harte) some what digressed, yet have I not utterlie forgotten my former proposition.'[3] And so he goes on in his Jeremiad, though he conceded his 'rude vehemencie and inconsidered affirmations, which may appear rather to procead from choler then of zeal and reason'.[4] To the charge of extremism he replies summarily 'to me it is yneugh to say, that black is not whit, and man's tyrannye and foolishnes is not Goddes perfite ordinance',[5] which of course for Knox settled the matter.

Again in this pamphlet Knox turns scholasticism against itself: 'to the most parte of men, lawfull and godlie appeareth whatsoever antiquitie hath received'.[6] To that Knox opposes the revolutionary demands of God's word.

(*Certain Tractates . . . by Ninian Winzet*, ed. J. K. Hewison. Scottish Text Society, Edinburgh, 1888, i. 138: Knox, *Works*, iv. 439). Cf. O. Sprotte, *Zum Sprachgebrauch bei John Knox*. Berlin, 1906: much work on this subject is still needed.

    [1] Knox, *op. cit.*, iv. 373.   [2] *Ibid.*, iv. 368.   [3] *Ibid.*, iv. 396.
    [4] *Ibid.*, v. 5.   [5] *Ibid.*   [6] *Ibid.*, iv. 370.

We have seen then Knox as pastor, theologian, political pamphleteer, a tender, gentle friend, a patient expositor, a shrewd diplomat, a highly skilled orator, a vehement impatient opponent, a bitter acid-tongued enemy, all by turns. We now come to the work in which all these qualities are merged, and on which the greatness of Knox the writer finally rests.

In May 1559 the Protestant leaders in Scotland recalled Knox from exile to help them to achieve the long-awaited establishment of a new church. To justify their policy and his own actions he wrote *The History of the Reformation of Religion in Scotland*, now in five books of which the first four were completed in Knox's life-time, not in their numerical order, but as II, III, I, IV. Book V contains enough to show that Knox had drafted considerable passages but its final form is due to some unknown writer.

It is not altogether easy to characterise the work. It is history in so far as it narrates events in their sequence and in the logic of their antecedents and the human motives that tried to control them—it gives the sources for its facts, liberally quoting from documents and referring to statements that can be verified from elsewhere—and later research has upheld Knox's general accuracy in this—but in the sense that it is a dispassionate account, designed to give a clear and composite view of *all* the causes and effects, it is not history at all nor does it claim to be. It is explicitly a partisan statement, a piece of propaganda, dealing only with religious affairs and not the civil polity generally and designed to counteract the arguments of the French party that the Reformers meant rebellion and to justify the action of the Lords of the Congregation in calling help from England. The reader is warned by the author himself that his judgment of the various characters is entirely determined by their attitude to the Reformed cause at any given time.[1] His *History* is in fact a volume of selective and frequently impressionistic memoirs, a species of composition in which Scottish writers have always been remarkably good, from Lindsay of Pitscottie and the two James Melvilles to Cockburn and Stevenson, and Knox is one of the most outstanding of them all.

Granted its self-confessed limitations, his *History* is a picture of his times which for depth of insight, brilliance of presentation and animation of style could hardly be bettered, and though

---

[1] Knox, *op. cit.*, i. 5.

critics have censured the slabs of documentation which break up the flow of the narrative, Knox's genius and single-minded dedication to his one theme, the triumph of the Reformation against all odds and vicissitides, give his story compelling dramatic force and unity. For Knox it was, *mutatis mutandis*, the drama of the Old Testament re-enacted in Scotland, with himself as Moses, Joshua, Isaiah, Jeremiah, Ezekiel, and Daniel rolled into one. The *History* is the ἀγών or struggle between great forces, Catholicism versus Protestantism, State versus Church, Monarchy versus People, future versus past, revolution versus reaction, at the point of no return and when no compromise remained possible, a situation in many ways like that of our own present day. But against the backcloth of national and international drama, there is the drama of Knox himself. In the midst of greater conflicts, we see the timid studious notary of Haddington, confronted by the tragedy of Wishart, drawn almost accidentally into the heart of the fray, and finally committed irrevocably to his destiny by the challenge to preach in St Andrews and the agonising soul-searching till he found what the Covenanters of the seventeenth century called 'outgate'; and so through the misery of the galleys, the euphoric days in King Edward's England, the years of study and reflection abroad when he was nerving himself for the crisis of his return to a Scotland in the grip of civil war; and finally in Book IV the climax of the drama in the confrontations with Queen Mary, and with Lethington in the trial scene before the Privy Council.

Not of course that Knox conceived his *History* in such literary terms as I may have suggested. The dramatic effect is not the result of conscious art or premeditation but of intensity of emotion from the experience of events dramatic in themselves recollected and recorded, but not in tranquillity. In the first two books written, i.e., II and III, he is nearest to the conventional historian, his bias apart, in giving an ostensibly temperate and objective account of things. He never obtrudes himself, and always speaks of himself in the third person. As a narrator, he has an eye to the essentials of a scene. There is for example the ring of realism in the story as we stand in the crowd with Knox watching the burning of the Abbey of Scone and overhear with him 'a poore aged matrone, seing the flambe of fyre pas up sa michtelie, and perceaving that many war thairat offended, ... said,

"Now I see and understand that Goddis judgementis ar just, and that no man is able to save whare he will punische. Since my remembrance, this place hath bein nothing ellis bot a den of hooremongaris. It is incredible to beleve how many wyffes hath bein adulterat, and virginis deflored, by the filthie beastis which hath bein fostered in this den; bot especiallie by that wicked man who is called the Bischope. Yf all men knew alsmuche as I, thay wald praise God; and no man wald be offended" '.[1] He is, surprisingly enough for an ex-priest, very good at battles, not so much in the actual fighting as in the psychological atmosphere, the arguments for this or that plan, the scurrying to and fro, the conflicting ambitions, the frequent half-heartedness, the confusion and panic, as for instance in his descriptions of Solway Moss and Pinkie in Book I, or of the Protestant debacle at the Siege of Leith in Book II, where he makes no attempt to conceal his disgust at the poltroonery of some of the Congregation and the pell-mell scramble to escape when the alarm was raised.

It was on the heels of this disaster that Knox preached what was probably his greatest sermon, as padre-in-chief to the army, at Stirling. It was a morale booster, full of parallels from the defeats of the Israelites and their ultimate triumph. Much of it is good old-fashioned stuff. 'Applying these headis to the tyme and personis, . . . yf none of Goddis children had suffered befoir us the same injureis that presentlie we susteane, these our trubles wald appear intollerable; suche is our tender delicacie, and self luif of our awin flesche, that those thingis which we lychtlie pass over in otheris, we can greatlie complane of, yf thei tweiche our selfis. . . . But whiche of us, eather in reading or hearing thair dolouris and temptationis, did so discend in to oure selfis that we felt the bitterness of thair passionis? I think none. And thairfoir hes God brocht us to some experience in our awin personis'[2] (there is a curious modern ring and applicability of that),—and then the trumpet again sounded the note we first heard in the Letter to the Congregation of St Andrews: 'Whatsoever shall become of us and our mortall carcasses. I dowt not but that this caus, (in dyspite of Satan,) shall prevaill in the realme of Scotland. For, as it is the eternall trewth of the eternall God, so shall it ones prevaill, howsoever for a time it be impugned.'[3]

---

[1] Knox, *op. cit.*, i. 361–2.   [2] *Ibid.*, i. 469.
[3] *Ibid.*, i. 472–3.

But God that could work great wonders over all nations, operated in small things too, and Knox in one of what he calls his 'merry' moods of rather grim humour tells of a French soldier looting a poor woman's beef-tub in Leith. 'The poore woman perceving him so bent, and that he stouped doun in hir tub, for the taking foorth of suche stufe as was within it, first cowped up his heillis, so that his heid went doun; and thairefter outher by hirself, or if ony uther cumpanie come to help hir, but thair he endit his unhappie lyfe; God so punissing his crewell hairt, quho could nocht spair a miserable woman in that extremitie.'[1]

In Book III we have an account of the siege of Leith which reminds one of Livy or Sallust, who were a popular authors in mediaeval Scotland. Then he tells, with due dramatic irony, of the death of the Queen Regent who when she was dying had asked her Lords for a clergyman and they had sent her Willock, Knox's colleague in St Giles', 'Albeit before sche had avowit, that in dyspite of all Scotland, the prechearis of Jesus Christ sould ather die or be banischeid the realme; yitt was sche compellit not onlie to heir that Chryst Jesus was precheit, and all idolatrie oppinlie rebuikit, and in many placeis suppressit, bot alssua sche was constraineit to heir ane of the principall ministeris within the realme, and to approve the cheif heid of oure religioun, quhairin we dissent frome all Papistis and Papistrie'.[2] More succinctly we have the same irony in his comment on the King of France, Mary, Queen of Scots' husband, who died of an abscess in his ear—'in that deaf eare that never wald hear the treuth of God'.[3]

Having brought the narrative to the Parliament of 1560 which established the Reformation and having added the Book of Discipline as the charter and articles of the new Church, Knox seems to have paused in his memoirs for some three years. In the meantime he had seen victory turned to ashes, the wealth, the patrimony as he called it, of the old Church diverted from his schemes for the education of the young and the care of the poor by the rapacity of the nobility; he had quarrelled with Moray, in whom he had pinned all his hopes, about royal authority; and he could see the Counter-Reformation gathering ominous strength after the Council of Trent in 1563. It was a soured and embittered

[1] Knox, *op. cit.*, ii. 15.   [2] *Ibid.* ii. 71.   [3] *Ibid.*, ii. 134.

Knox that resumed his *History* with Book I in 1566. It was ostensibly meant to tell the story of the Protestant martyrs, Hamilton, Wishart, etc., and his writing reflects the moods aroused by the events as he remembered them, hope, despair, humour, exasperation, bitterness and rancour, the last exacerbated by his own gloom about the future. Nowhere does Knox reveal his own character more fully, warts and all, than in the first and last books of the *History*, and, whether one approves or not of Knox, it should be remembered that most of the evidence against as well as for him comes from the candour of his own writing.

His rhetorical skill is given full scope when his feelings carry him away. He is reasonably dispassionate in his sketch of King James V.—'All men lamented that the realme was left without a male to succeid; yit some rejosed that such ane ennemy to Goddis treuth was taekin away. He was called of some, a good poore manis King; of otheris hie was termed a murtherare of the nobilitie, and one that had decreed thair hole destructioun. Some prased him for the repressing of thyft and oppressioun; otheris disprased him for the defoulling of menis wyffis and virgines. And thus men spak evin as affectionis led theme'[1]—as Knox himself did. He was less charitable to James's daughter. 'She was sold to go to France, to the end that in hir youth she should drynk of that lycour, that should remane with hir all hir lyfetyme, for a plague to this realme, and for hir finall destructioun. . . . [God shall] eyther destroy that hoore in hir hurdome, or ellis he shall putt it in the hartis of a multitude, to tak the same vengeance upoun hir, that hes bein tane of Jesabell and Athalia.'[2] Strong intemperate words, written however when Mary was in the midst of her amour with the man who had murdered her husband about six weeks before, and was riding headlong for disaster. Like it or not, our prophet was proved sadly right again.

For contrast of moods one can compare his treatment of the episode of Wishart with that of the murder of Cardinal Beaton. There is a curiously haunting power in his description of Wishart at Haddington when he saw the net closing round him, with faint echoes of the Gethsemane story which Knox returns to again and again even to his deathbed; there was Wishart's wild and despairing outburst of prophecy and denunciation, which Knox was to repeat so often throughout his own preaching; and

[1] Knox, *op. cit.*, i. 92–93.   [2] *Ibid.*, i. 218.

finally the calm after the storm, when he heard Wishart's last words to him, 'Nay, returne to your barnes, and God blisse yow. One is sufficient for a sacrifice'.[1]

For Beaton, however, there is no compassion—merely mordant scorn—'The Cardinall's graceless Grace, the carnall Cardinall' sitting in his 'Babylone', his new Castle 'where he was suyre, as he thought';[2] Kirkcaldy of Grange asking the porter ' "Yf My Lord was walking?" who ansuered, "No". (And so it was in dead; for he had bene busy at his comptis with Maistres Marioun Ogilvye that nycht.)'[3]

The sarcasm is somewhat more delicate but equally cutting in regard to the Earl of Bothwell (Mary's Bothwell's father) who betrayed Wishart. 'As gold and wemen have corrupted all worldlye and fleschlye men from the begynning, so did thei him. For the Cardinall gave gold, and that largelye, and the Quene, with whome the said Erle was then in the glondouris, promissed favouris in all his lauchfull suyttis to wemen, yf he wold deliver the said Maister George to be keap in the Castell of Edinburgh. He made some resistance at the first, be reassone of his promesse; butt ane effeminat man cane not long withstand the assaultes of a gratious Quein.'[4] Knox is a master of innuendo. He can be briefer and even more trenchant in striking off a character with little more than a stroke of a very barbed pen, and in this he reminds us of yet another Roman historian and rhetorician, Tacitus himself, as when he says of the Bishop of Brechin: 'blynd of ane eie in the body, and of boithe in his saule';[5] of Lord Seton: 'a man without God, without honestie, and often-tymes without reasone';[6] of Lady Erskine: 'a sweate morsall for the devill's mouth',[7] which may of course be a left-handed compliment; of Mary of Guise, when she was made Regent, 'als seimlye a sight . . . as to putt a sadill upoun the back of ane unrewly kow';[8] of the Bishop of Ross: he died 'eatting and drynking, which, togitther with the rest that tharupoun dependis, was the pastyme of his lyef'.[9]

He is at home too in more slap-stick comedy, in the rough-and-tumble humour of brawls and scuffles, in the good old *Christ's Kirk* and *Peblis to the Play* tradition in Scottish literature, as in

---

[1] Knox, *op. cit.* i. 139. [2] *Ibid.*, i. 172. [3] *Ibid.*, i. 174.
[4] *Ibid.*, i. 143. [5] *Ibid.*, i. 235. [6] *Ibid.*, i. 362–3.
[7] *Ibid.*, ii. 380. [8] *Ibid.*, i. 242. [9] *Ibid.*, i. 263.

the fight for precedence among the clergy outside Glasgow
Cathedral, when 'rockettis war rent, typpetis war torne, crounis
war knapped. . . . Many of thame lacked beardis, and that was the
more pitie; and tharefore could not bukkill other by the byrse,
as bold men wold haif doune'.[1] Or in a later fracas in Edinburgh
when a Protestant mob set on the churchmen parading the image
of St Giles: 'The Gray Freiris gapped, the Blak Frearis blew, the
Preastis panted, and fled, and happy was he that first gate the
house.'[2]

But Knox's humour is not always unfeeling and in his story of
the French poet, Châtelard, he conveys not a little of the pathos of
the whole affair though of course he uses it as a stick against Mary.
In dancing 'the Quene chosed Chattelett, and Chattelett took the
Quene. . . . The Quene wold ly upoun Chattelettis shoulder, and
sometymes prively she wold steal a kyss of his neck. And all this
was honest yneuch; for it was the gentill entreatment of a stranger.
But the familiaritie was so great, that upon a nycht, he privelie
did convey him self under the Quenis bed; but being espyed, he
was commanded away. . . . the Quene called the Erle of Murray,
. . . and charged him . . . [that] he should slay Chattelett, and let
him never say word'. Moray demurred, suggesting rather that
Châtelard should be put on trial in a regular manner. So 'poor
Chattelett was brocht back from Kinghorne to Sanctandrois,
examinat, putt to ane assise, and so beheaded. . . . At the place of
executioun, when he saw that thair was no remeady but death,
he maid a godly confessioun and granted, that his declining from
the treuth of God, and following of vanitie and impietie, was
justlie recompensed upoun him. But in the end he concluded,
looking unto the heavenis, with these words, "O cruelle Dame."
. . . What that complaint imported, luvaris may devine. And so
receaved Chattelett the reward of his dansing; for he lacked his
head, that his toung should nott utter the secreattis of our Quene.
"Deliver us, O Lord, from the raige of such inordinat reullaris." '[3]

But the interest of Book IV must remain finally in the four
dramatic confrontations between Knox and the Queen—dramatic
in the penetrating analysis and the clash of personalities as well
as of principles, and these we have to discuss not for their
substance (which is not my brief) but for their setting in Knox's
historical play.

---

[1] Knox, *op. cit.*, i. 147.   [2] *Ibid.*, i. 260.   [3] *Ibid.*, ii. 367–8.

The first argument, after some preliminary fencing about the Mass, got round to the question of royal authority where Mary drove Knox into reasserting the theories of *The First Blast* and the *Admonition* on the duty and right of subjects to rebel against a ruler who forced what Knox called idolatry on her subjects. He on the other hand got Mary to say that for her the Church of Rome was the only true Church. Thus we see the stage set for the two protagonists on their collision course; and with his comment: 'Yf thair be not in hir . . . a proud mynd, a crafty witt, and ane indurat heatred against God and his treuth, my judgment faileth me', Knox subtly prepares us for the next encounter.[1]

That, though a much slighter affair, marks the intensification of the struggle. Knox had preached against dancing at Court, not so much *qua* dancing but because he suspected that the dance was to celebrate the defeat of the Huguenots in France. If, said Mary, Knox had anything to complain of in her behaviour, let him come to her privately, to which Knox retorted that he was not her confessor, but a public preacher, whose place was in the pulpit. Let her Majesty attend St Giles', if she wished to hear God's doctrine. In effect Mary and Knox were fighting for control of propaganda. Knox felt he had got the best of the argument and even made one of his rare pleasant jokes when asked if he was not afraid of the Queen: 'Why should the pleasing face of a gentill woman effray me?'[2] And it should be noted that in the royal presence he always couched the utmost defiance in the most courteous tones. But the issues are becoming clearer, and the knives sharper.

The third interview at Loch Leven is the calm before the storm, but the calm of increasing tension. Mary went out of her way to be pleasant, Knox was guarded but deferential, but Mary failed to get Knox's co-operation in preventing a clash between Protestants and Catholics in the West, and Knox was edged ever nearer the position of rebellion. If the Government will not enforce the law, the people must do it for themselves. Once again the modernity of the situation must strike us.

It was at the fourth interview that the storm broke, over a sermon by Knox against the Queen's proposed marriage with one or other Catholic prince. It was on this occasion that the

[1] Knox, *op. cit.*, ii. 286.   [2] *Ibid.*, ii. 335.

Queen burst into tears, more of exasperation than grief, and the two sides of Knox's character come into play at once, the gentle Knox rather awkwardly apologising for having upset her, and the relentless Knox who as a man would willingly offend no one, but in the preaching-place: 'I am nott maister of my self, but man obey Him who commandis me to speik plane, and to flatter no flesche upoun the face of the earth.'[1]

This of course is one of the immortal scenes in Scottish history, the very essence of drama. We with our hindsight know that the one died in peace in a vision of Gethsemane, the other on a scaffold with her crucifix in her hand; we see them as the dedicated victims of the tempests of history and of forces beyond themselves that drove them inexorably on.

But Knox has his last word in the long tedious semi-scriptural wrangle with Lethington with which Book IV ends. Maitland seems to have been looked upon as the chief theorist in Scotland of absolute monarchy and you will remember Buchanan's fictitious dialogue between Maitland and himself in the *De Jure Regni*. Like most arguments it got nowhere, but Knox managed to make his point on which he had taken his stand ten years before: 'Godis pepill hes executit Godis law aganis their King' and may do so again, 'whair the lyke crymes ar committit'.[2] Or to put it in Ridley's succinct words: 'The theory of the justification of revolution is Knox's special contribution to theological and political thought.'[3]

Of Knox the Writer then we can say that he wrote as vehemently and dramatically as he lived. He was essentially a man of words, a rhetorician, a committed, astute and determined propagandist for what he believed in. Whether that was a good or bad thing, it is not the province of this talk to discuss. He was at least on the winning side and the results for Scotland are still with us. Whatever we think of Knox's achievement, he is far too great to be ignored, and too vital and too relevant to be indifferent to.

---

[1] Knox, *op. cit.*, ii. 387.   [2] *Ibid.*, ii. 453.   [3] Ridley, *Knox.* 171.

John Knox and Mary, Queen of Scots

The Reverend DUNCAN SHAW, Ph.D., Th.Dr.

*Minister of the Parish of Craigentinny, Edinburgh and
Secretary of the General Council of the University of Edinburgh*

To many, this paper may appear to be merely another recounting of an old theme and some, in face of the immense bibliography on Mary Stuart,[1] may question the necessity of adding further to the subject. Nevertheless, Knox and Mary, representing two distinctly differing movements, as well as possessing entirely different personal attributes and outlooks, are worthy of a reappraisal in view of much that has been written before and since the last consideration of their relationships.[2] All would admit, with that most self-effacing of historians, W. H. Marwick, that 'on the "lunatic fringe" on either side we have indeed still such utterances as that of a High Church clergyman, that "the Scottish Reformation was a hell-hatched conspiracy", and the counter view attributed to a Free Kirk minister, who ranked it with the Creation and the Resurrection as the three great events of world history. And hack writers will no doubt continue to cater for the romantic interest which has bedevilled Scottish history, by publishing volumes devoted to mariolatry of a far from virgin queen or to hero worshipping panegyrics of John Knox.'[3] The historian's point of departure has changed. He no longer assumes that matters of faith and developments within the church can be isolated from world movements and non-theological concepts. He is now much less motivated by pre-conceptions or dogmatical presuppositions and, in the realm of

[1] S. and M. Tannenbaum, *Maria Stuart. Bibliography*. New York, 1944. 3 vols.

[2] H. Watt, *John Knox in Controversy*. Edinburgh, 1950. 69–106: cf. G. Donaldson's review in *S.H.R.*, xxx. 182–6 and A. Ross's review in *The Innes Review*, i. 161–2.

[3] W. M. Marwick, 'The Scottish Reformation: A Quaker Commentary on Recent Literature', in *The Friends' Quarterly*. London, 1960. 341.

Reformation studies, he has learned of such dangers not only from the products of past ecclesiastical historical myopy but also from those of contemporary Marxist schematic historians.[1]

Before any attempt can be made to understand the relationship which existed between Mary, Queen of Scots and John Knox, some attention must be paid to the ways in which their personalities and ideas developed long before they ever met. The clashes which took place between them are important, not because of the great interest which has been shown in their meetings, but because they particularise many of the conflicting streams of thought which confronted each other with growing intensity and which have continued to do so for centuries.

When Mary landed in Scotland, what did she think about herself? She came as Queen from a country where the sycophantic doctrine of kingship was gaining ground. The mediaeval ideas and legends about the French kings were still powerful—'like the royal miracle of healing scrofula by touch,[2] like the Holy Vial containing celestial balm for anointing the king, like the Oriflamme, or the golden lilies'.[3] Such ideas were alien to Scotland, as was her view of society which was completely hierarchical and had been safeguarded in France by repression.

On her return to Leith from France, she was not taken to the house of any of the nobility but was given hospitality by a local burgess. In the evening, when she reached Edinburgh, she was immediately aware that the cultural and social setting in which she had grown up was vastly different from that of the Scottish court. When a comparison is made between the architecture of the magnificent palaces which had been built in France[4] and the bleak primitiveness of those in Scotland, an almost psychological shock could await a young woman moving from one to the other at the impressionable age of eighteen. There can be added to this the innumerable servants, the varieties of food and drink, the music and dancing, the clothing and jewellery, the furniture,

[1] Cf. e.g., *450 Jahre Reformation*, edd. L. Stern and M. Steinmetz. Berlin, 1967. For a discussion of the whole matter cf. H-G. Koch, *Luthers Reformation in kommunistischer Sicht*. Stuttgart, 1967, particularly 210–22.

[2] M. Bloch, *Les Rois Thaumaturges, étude sur le caractère surnaturel attribué à la puissance royale particulièrement en France et en Angleterre*. Paris, 1924.

[3] E. H. Kantorowicz, *Laudes Regiae. A Study in Liturgical Acclamations and Mediaeval Ruler Worship*. Berkley and Los Angeles, 1958. 3.

[4] A. Blunt, *Art and Architecture in France. 1500–1700*. London, 1953.

tapestries, paintings and books, the gardens, the coaches—all the magnificence of an imperial power of several millions compared with the poverty of a people of five hundred thousand.[1]

To complete the awesome impression, the populace of Edinburgh turned out in considerable force to sing psalms to the Queen on her first evening in Holyrood. Although Knox records that she liked the melody well and 'willed the same to be continued some nights after',[2] her diplomacy was guiding her, not the unnerving recollections of psalm-singing in France where the Protestant crowds had often assembled for psalm-singing as a public demonstration against the authorities.[3]

Above all, the main fear which Mary had to face within herself was the possibility of a breakdown of law and order within the realm and, considering herself to be at the summit of the hierarchical pyramid of society, she sensed that for her the primary sin tempting Scotland was the same as that identified by scholastic theology namely disorder.[4]

Even before Mary set foot in Scotland, she undoubtedly had already a picture in her mind of the person of Knox with whom she knew instinctively she would have difficulties. In the first place, from the highest stratum of society, she observed a peasant with whom she would have to deal. When one remembers that W. H. Riehl found after exhaustive research that the German peasant farmer of a century ago had a vocabulary of only six hundred words,[5] one can imagine the cultural expectations which Mary had of a man sprung from a background more primitive than that investigated by Riehl. Yet, in her own eyes, there were far more serious defects. He was not only a renegade priest, he had been degraded from holy orders and, as one who had been sentenced to death in an ecclesiastical court, he had no legal existence. Facts, that had made even the Lords of the Congregation temper their actions not long before Mary's arrival in

---

[1] Pierre de Bourdeilles, Abbé de Brantône, *Vies des femmes illustres,* ed. L. Moland. Nouvelle édition. Paris. n.d. 117f.

[2] Knox, *History,* ii. 8.

[3] W. S. Reid, 'The Battle Hymns of the Lord: Calvinist Psalmody of the Sixteenth Century', in *Sixteenth Century Essays and Studies,* ed. C. S. Meyer. St Louis, Missouri, 1971, ii. 36–54.

[4] Thomas Aquinas, *Summa Theologica,* II, 1 82, 3 quoted by G. W. Locher, *Huldrych Zwingli in neuer Sicht.* Zürich, 1969. 29n and comments there.

[5] Quoted by G. G. Coulton, *The Medieval Village.* Cambridge, 1925. 65.

Scotland.[1] Mary probably also took fairly seriously the rumours
that he was not only a heretic but a necromancer.[2] This confusion
of magic and heresy, no doubt, reflected an attitude of mind
which had been common in Europe since the inauguration by
Pope John XXII in 1326 of a series of witch trials in southern
France and found an echo in the promulgation by Pope Adrian
VI in 1523 of a Bull in which excommunication was directed
against sorcerers and heretics.[3] Many considered the terms almost
synonomous. However, in her assessment of Knox as a man against
all female government, a seditious rabble-rouser and one committed to revolution by force, she was prepared to see that all
this did not spring from the black arts and it is fairly certain that
she believed she had personal charming qualities which would
enable her to wheedle something out of this complex, intriguing
character.

Knox himself was unaware of the complexities within his own
person. He was convinced of his divine prophetic ministry which
had commenced with the call he had received from the castillians
of St Andrews.[4] He knew himself to be 'called of my God to
instruct the ignorant, comfort the sorrowful, confirm the weak,
and rebuke the proud, by tongue and lively voice in these most
corrupt days, . . . I dare not deny (lest that in so doing I should be
injurious to the giver), but that God hath revealed unto me
secrets unknown to the world; and also that he made my tongue
a trumpet, to forewarn realms and nations, yea, certain great
personages, of translations and changes, when no such things
were feared, nor yet was appearing, a portion whereof cannot
the world deny (be it never so blind) to be fulfilled; and the rest,
alas! I fear, shall follow with greater expedition, and in more full
perfection, than my sorrowful heart desireth. These revelations
and assurances notwithstanding, I did ever abstain to commit
anything to writ, contented only to have obeyed the charge of
Him who commanded me to cry.'[5]

[1] Knox, *History*, i. 181.

[2] For the general background: cf. W. Shumaker, *The Occult Sciences in the
Renaissance*. Berkley, 1972.

[3] H. C. E. Midelfort, *Witch Hunting in South Western Germany. 1562–1684*.
London, 1972.

[4] Knox, *History*, i. 82–83. This is a different concept of prophecy to that
of the mediaeval era: cf. H. Reeves, *The Influence of Prophecy in the Later
Middle Ages*. Oxford, 1972.   [5] Knox, *Works*, vi. 229–30.

While most Scots in 1560 would not, in spite of Geddes MacGregor's claim, have thought of Knox as 'the Moses of the Scots, their Amos and their Isaiah too',[1] Knox considered himself to have been just that or, rather than Moses, 'the Joshua of the Scots', for Moses never entered the promised land. Knox, like Joshua, did. With the Reformation, the promised land lay before every Scot. This is made clear in his speech to the General Assembly of June, 1564: 'For I speak of the people assembled together in one body of the Commonwealth, and to whom God has given sufficient force, not only to resist but also to suppress all kind of open idolatry: and such a people yet again I affirm, are bound to keep their land clean and unpolluted. And that this division shall not appear strange unto you, ye shall understand that God required one thing of Abraham and his seed when he and they were strangers and pilgrims in Egypt and Canaan; and another thing required he of them when they were delivered from the bondage of Egypt, and the possession of the land of Canaan was granted unto them.'[2]

The achievements had to be safeguarded. Knox was well aware of the danger of the Reformers' position being lost to alien forces without or because of a lethargy of the faithful in firmly establishing their position at home. God's promise had been fulfilled but his fears were the same as Calvin's which were expressed about the same time in Geneva in his comments on the Book of Joshua, 'it was owing entirely to their own cowardice that they did not enjoy the divine goodness in all its fulness and integrity'[3]. 'It is necessary,' said Calvin, 'to distinguish between the certain, clear, and steadfast faithfulness of God in keeping his promises, and between the effeminacy and sluggishness of the people, in consequence of which the benefit of the divine goodness in a manner slipped through their hands.'[4]

John Knox was determined that this would not be the case with the commonwealth in Scotland.

Even before Mary's return to Scotland, Knox had certain ideas about her firmly fixed in his mind. The death of her husband, Francis II, had been 'a wonderful and most joyful deliverance'

[1] G. MacGregor, *The Thundering Scot*. London, 1960. 44.
[2] Knox, *History*, ii. 122.
[3] J. Calvin, *Commentaries on the Book of Joshua*, trans. H. Beveridge. Edinburgh, 1854. 248.   [4] *Ibid.*

to him.[1] This natural annulment of his receipt of the crown
matrimonial put an end to legal French constitutional intervention
in Scotland, but much was not changed because of this. Knox
was conscious of the influence of the Guise family upon the
Queen. The lessons of the Cardinal of Lorraine were, in Knox's
view, 'so deeply imprinted upon her heart that the substance and
quality were like to perish together'[2] and he had no difficulty in
describing her other uncle, François de Lorraine, Duke of Guise,
as a 'bloody tyrant'.[3]

Yet the chief defect in Mary was her adherence to the Mass.
This marked her out as the inspiration for a return to past
idolatries and the vanguard of all reactionary policies, including
the undermining of the Protestant government in England.

The idolatry of the Mass was closely related in the mind of
Knox, as with many others in Scotland, to moral instability. He
classed massmongering and immorality together as the town
council of Edinburgh did in a proclamation of 2 October 1561,
when reference is made to 'all monks, friars, priests, nuns,
adulterers, fornicators and all such filthy persons'.[4] Within weeks
of Mary's arrival in Scotland, her gay court parties, her own
behaviour at them and her somewhat free behaviour with certain
male courtiers, and particularly her dancing, seemed to indicate to
Knox a certain propensity towards the practices of the fertility
cult of Canaan much in the same way as the Mass was but a
repetition of the abominations practised in the promised land
before the children of Israel took possession.[5]

It should, however, be remembered, that Knox's views on
dancing were no different to the general position of the mediaeval
church nor the Roman church after the Reformation.[6]

He would have had his worst fears confirmed if he had been
aware of Mary's interest in such literature as the *Decameron*[7] or the

[1] Knox, *History*, i. 347.

[2] Knox, *Works*, vi. 132.   [3] Knox, *History*, ii. 84.

[4] *Extracts from the Records of the Burgh of Edinburgh. 1557–1571*, ed. J. D.
Marwick. Scottish Burgh Record Society, Edinburgh, 1875. 125.

[5] Knox, *History*, ii. 330–5.

[6] G. G. Coulton, *The Medieval Village*. Cambridge, 1925. 558–63: G. G.
Coulton, *Five Centuries of Religion*. Cambridge, 1929, i. 531–8.

[7] *Inuentaires de la royne descosse douairiere de France. 1556–1569*, ed.
J. Robertson. Bannatyne Club, Edinburgh, 1863 (later referred to as
Inuentaires). cvi.

novels of Rabelais[1] who, in spite of his anti-clericalism, was considered beyond the pale by Reformers and Roman Catholics alike.

John Prebble has dogmatically declaimed that John Knox's 'great hatreds were never spoiled by small compassions'.[2] We will learn that his behaviour shows him to be otherwise and, when one reads all that Knox said about Mary in anger, fear or frustration, even before he met her, and bearing in mind his own tendency to be attracted by women a good deal younger than himself, the impression remains that there was a certain response in him to that fascination which many found exerted upon them by Mary, Queen of Scots.

Before considering in detail the meetings which took place between Knox and Mary, it is necessary to remember that, although there are references in a number of sources, the only record of any great significance, concerning the confrontations, are given by Knox himself. It is noticeable that he gives his own contributions to the debate in considerable detail compared to the questions put by Mary and her responses to some of his statements.

It could be suggested that Knox, in his *History of the Reformation in Scotland*, was only concerned to record what his own views were and gave a mere sketch of what the Queen had to say when they faced each other. Yet, knowing the attitudes of Mary, it would seem likely that the account which Knox gives, is, in all probability, fairly accurate. Mary was concerned to learn Knox's views at first hand and was not prepared to demean herself by debating at length with him as an equal, nor was she willing to state her personal opinions in case she gave the impression that she was prepared to enter into personal negotiations with him.

In these circumstances, it has been necessary to attempt to glean from other sources the ideas that influenced her and to strive to reconstruct the attitudes that she had adopted when she summoned John Knox before her.

The first meeting of Knox and Mary occurred within two months of her arrival in Scotland and was the most significant of all their interviews as the problems referred to by Mary were the most important which divided not only them but Scotland itself.

---

[1] *Ibid.*, cviii. There was, of course, another side to Rabelais, cf. M. Screech, *L'Évangelisme de Rabelais*. Geneva, 1959.

[2] J. Prebble, *The Lion in the North*. London, 1971. 190.

Mary's fundamental concern was to clarify in her own mind Knox's attitude to her authority in politics and religion.

When Mary accused Knox of raising part of the country against her mother and herself, it is certain that she was incapable of going to the heart of the constitutional problem because her ideas were totally alien to the influences exerted upon Knox which were unknown to her.

Although it is not possible to rehearse in detail, within the compass of this paper, all the political opinions of Knox, it is sufficient to say that the significance of Knox's mentioning the *Confession Instruction and Warning of the Pastors and Preachers of the Christian Churches of Magdeburg*, 1550 (*Bekenntnis Unterricht und Vermahnung der Pfarherrn und Prediger der Christlichen Kirchen zu Magdeburg*) can only now be appreciated.[1] It was inspired by the teaching of the Torgau *Gutachten* of October 1531 signed by Luther, Jonas, Melanchthon and Spalatin which recognised the legitimacy of armed resistance of the lesser magistrates if it were carried out in accordance with the provisions of the imperial law;[2] and Andreas Osiander later expressed the opinion that the term lesser magistrates included city government who if acting lawfully could resist a sinful emperor.

The *Confession of Magdeburg* however was the document which crystallised the doctrine that 'the lesser magistrates' had a God-given duty under certain circumstances to take up arms against the higher authority. This document, coming from a city which had faced a long siege but had been able to retain its freedom of religion against the Emperor, transmitted this Lutheran teaching to Scotland. The doctrine propounded had the capacity to fit the needs of Knox and others of having a legally and theologically based doctrine of resistance.

As has been said, 'The Protestant theory of political resistance by inferior magistrates, far from being a mere rationalization for an essentially feudal resistance, as has sometimes been suggested, was rather the locus of one of the Protestants' most notable

---

[1] J. W. Allen, *A History of Political Thought in the Sixteenth Century*, rev. ed., London, 1957, 106: does not confidently connect the *Bekenntnis* with the *Apology* but it was certainly the *Bekenntnis*, as a comparison with the Latin title proves.

[2] *D. Martin Luthers Werke, Briefwechsel*. Weimar, 1930f (later referred to to as *W.A.Br.*). vi. 405–6.

fusions of "medieval" and "modern", the creation of a theory of government in which the king, feudal officials, royal magistrates and estates were all regarded as public officials with mutual obligations to censure each other in the name of justice and common weal. This was not yet a modern constitutional theory of government with rationally divided branches and departments and regularised modes of procedure, but the most advanced Protestant political thought did move in this direction from the more informal and uncertain means of limiting royal power in the Middle Ages.'[1]

It is significant that in the debate in the General Assembly of June 1564, while Knox commented and, to some extent refuted, the anti-resistance theories of William Maitland which the latter had founded on citations from Luther, Melanchthon, Bucer, Musculus and Calvin, Knox felt that he clinched the argument when he produced the *Confession of Magdeburg* and asked Maitland to read out the names of those who signed it, including Nicolaus von Amsdorf, bishop of Naumburg.[2]

Calvin had propounded similar views to Admiral Gaspard de Coligny in April 1561[3] doubtless also influenced by the *Confession of Magdeburg*, but it seems certain that Knox did not know the contents of the letter.

The doctrine of the power of the lesser magistrates, which was interpreted as including lords, lairds and burgesses, provided the ideological basis for the actions of the Lords of the Congregation. Within the Scottish constitution it was probably easier to move from theory to practice where the power of the crown had never been strong either in theory or in practice.[4]

Thus resistance was not revolution, it was the method to be used when every other means failed to secure legal rights. The way in which these rights were to be decided is outlined in 'The First Oration and Petition of the Protestants of Scotland to the

[1] R. Benert, 'Inferior Magistrates in Sixteenth Century Political and Legal Thought'. Unpublished Ph.D. thesis, University of Minnesota, 1967. ii.

[2] Knox, *History*, ii. 129–30.

[3] 'if the princes . . . demanded to be maintained in their rights for the common good, and if the Parliament joined them in their quarrel . . . it would be lawful for all good subjects to lend them armed resistance.' (*Letters of John Calvin*, ed. J. Bonnet. Philadelphia, 1858, iii. 176.)

[4] J. A. Lovat-Fraser, 'Constitutional Position of the Scottish Monarch prior to the Union', in *Law Quarterly Review*. Edinburgh, 1901, xvii. 252–62.

Queen Regent' of 1558. 'We are content,' the petitioners wrote, 'not only that the rules and precepts of the New Testament, but also the writings of the ancient Fathers, and the godly approved laws of Justinian the Emperor, decide the controversy betwixt us and [the prelates].'[1]

The reference to the Justinian Code reveals again the influence of the Lutherans. Appeal to the Code had been their practice since the issue of the *Gutachten* of 6 December 1536 by Luther, Jonas, Bugenhagen, Cruciger, Melanchthon and Amsdorf.[2]

A similar attitude to the place of Roman Law is shown in the coronation oath of 1567 when James VI promised to 'rule the people committed to their charge according to the will and command of God, revealed in his foresaid word, and according to the lovable Laws and constitutiouns received in this Realm, no wise repugnant to the said word of the eternal God'.[3]

Far from attempting to understand what Knox was saying, it was even impossible for Mary to grapple with the theories which lay behind his statements. She sprang from an entirely different world. She saw society much as Shakespeare allows Ulysses to describe it in *Troilus and Cressida*:

The heavens themselves, the planets and this centre,
Observe degree, priority, and place,
Insisture, course, proportion season, form,
Office, and custom, in all line of order;
.... O, when degree is shak'd,
Which is the ladder to all high designs,
The enterprise is sick! ....
Take but degree away, untune that string,
And, hark what discord follows! Each things melts
In mere oppugnancy: .....
And this neglection of degree it is
That by a pace backward, with a purpose
It hath to climb. The general's disdain'd
By him one step below, he by the next,
That next by him beneath; so every step,
Exampl'd by the first pace that is sick
Of his superior, grows to an envious fever
Of pale and bloodless emulation.[4]

[1] Knox, *History*, i. 151.   [2] *W.A.Br.*, vii. 604f.
[3] *A.P.S.*, iii. 23.   [4] *Troilus and Cressida*, i.iii. 85–134.

Not only did she conceive of society in the mediaeval hierarchical structure so well described by Johan Huizinga in his famous chapter in *The Waning of the Middle Ages*,[1] but she had an abhorrence of any form of sedition against the anointed sovereign. King Richard's words, again from Shakespeare, are an apt illustration of her views:

Not all the water in the rough rude sea
Can wash the balm off from an anointed king;[2]

For well we know no hand of blood and bone
Can gripe the sacred handle of our sceptre,
Unless he do profane, steal or usurp.[3]

Such concepts are supported by the political theorists—all French—whose works were in the Queen's library at Holyrood. There were two printed volumes, Guillaume de la Perrière, *Le Miroir politique*, Lyons, 1555; and Charles du Moulin, *Traité de l'origine, progrès et excellence du Royaume et Monarchie des Français*, Paris, 1561.[4]

Although Charles du Moulin's political theory undermined those supporting the feudal system, he, like Perrière, was a forerunner who developed the details of the divine right of kings. Du Moulin considered that if the king acted against the law of nature, which was considered to be synonymous with the word of God, he should not be obeyed[5] but the subject's only right of redress was to petition the ruler and be exonerated. His teaching generally 'resulted in the absorption of all personal relationships into the obligation of all men to serve the king . . . and the whole was focused so as to identify the policy and the profit of the king with the good of the state . . . In this fashion, du Moulin developed a complete social theory in which all men were subjects of a wise and paternal king and could but submit to his rule, not only because it resulted from his supreme and unshared authority over all but also because it was synonymous with the best interest of the state and represented justice itself . . . the ultimate effect of the direct subjection of all men to the monarch was to deny many rights which the populace had enjoyed under the earlier system

---

[1] Chapter III. The Hierarchial Conception of Society.
[2] *Richard II*, iii.ii. 54–55.   [3] *Ibid.*, iii.ii. 79–81.
[4] *Inuentaires*, cviii.   [5] *Traité*. 70.

[of feudalism].'[1] Du Moulin's work had been put on the Index but this did not affect in any way the influence he had in France.

The views of Guillaume de la Perrière were very similar. He also emphasised the need to conserve the existing social organisation. While he recognised that society contained various elements which performed distinctive functions within the whole, the king stood at the summit of the hierarchy and held solely in himself all governmental authority.[2] His prime duty was to preserve the existing structure of society; while one of his main responsibilities was to prevent sedition because it broke down the integral order of society and altered the delicate mechanism of its component parts. The fifth chapter of his *Le Miroir politique* is devoted to ways of preventing sedition. For him, the state and the law were unchangeable.

The other work in her library which was important for such considerations was a manuscript entitled 'On the government of Princes'.[3] It is most likely that this was connected to Guillaume Budé's manuscript of 1519 entitled 'De l'institution du Prince' and his *Enseignement et Exhortement pour l'Institution d'un Prince*, Paris (or Lyon), 1547. The theories of Budé, if anything, went further in absolutising the powers of the King and denying any possibility of judicial checks being exerted upon his actions. The king was a god among men and a law unto himself.[4] He laid great stress on the great dimension of the legitimate royal discretion and he was willing at times to draw a parallel between the French king and the Roman dictator.[5] The king alone is judge of what is equitable.[6] Two other authors whose works referred to the institution of Christian princes appeared in her library.[7]

Budé's absolutist views were the most attractive for Mary. She had a book of verses in French, 'De l'institution d'un Prince',

---

[1] W. F. Church, *Constitutional Thought in Sixteenth-Century France. A Study in the Evolution of Ideas.* Cambridge, USA, 1941. 193–4.

[2] *Le Miroir politique.* 22–26.

[3] *Inuentaires,* cxiv.

[4] *De l'institution du prince,* 7v–8r.

[5] *Ibid.,* 82r.

[6] *Enseignement,* cap. 30.

[7] Pierre Boaistuau, *L'Histoire de Chelidonius Tigurinus sur l'institution des princes chrétiens et origine des royaumes.* Paris, 1557; and Synesius, *L'Institution d'un Prince Chrétien,* trans. Daniel d'Ange. Paris, 1555.

which doubtlessly expounded Budé's theories, prepared as a gift for her son. James VI was later to declare that this was one of his most treasured heirlooms.

It is interesting that du Moulin and de la Perrière do not feature in his library but there were two copies of Budé's *Enseignement*.[1]

Against such a background, it is not surprising that Mary, in her interrogating of Knox, never received any answers which fitted into her pattern of thought.

It is important to note that when Knox answers Mary's questions concerning her authority he does not, in the first interview, refer to his claims to the validity of appealing to Justinian to ascertain whether or not there are grounds for lawful resistance. His avoidance of such a procedure probably arose because he knew that Mary would not have appreciated the point he was trying to make and, secondly, because recent developments in France had produced a fully developed apologia for absolutism based on a total ignoring of Roman Law. Such would be the basis of her thinking. As du Moulin wrote, 'It is certain that the King of France, sovereign Lord in his Kingdom, has no less power than had Justinian the Great or other emperors in their empire'.[2]

The basic debate which was really relevant to the situation was not resistance by the lower magistrates, although references were made to this in their meeting of April 1563 and Knox, while sub-scribing to it, transferred the argument to the possibility of some co-operation between Mary and the lesser magistrates. They had achieved the reform of the Church and the necessary legal enact-ments had already been made in the parliament of 1560 although they had not yet been ratified by the Queen. The fundamental problem was expressed by Mary in the question, 'ye have taught the people to receive another religion than their princes can allow. And how can that doctrine be of God, seeing that God commands subjects to obey their princes?'[3] Mary possibly did not realise that her idea that subjects must have the same religion as their rulers was no longer universally accepted. The peace treaty of

[1] *Misc. S.H.S.*, i. xli, lvi (one of which was given by Lady Atholl, most probably Margaret, third daughter of Malcolm, third Earl of Fleming, wife of the fourth Earl of Atholl and sister of Mary Fleming).

[2] Moulin, *Traité*. 68.

[3] Knox, *History*, ii. 16.

Magdeburg had become a precedent for such an outlook. Mary's question also revealed that she was in no way influenced by the suggestion made in one of the French books in her library[1] that the state of the Church required the establishment of two churches in France and that there was no reason why such an arrangement should not be made.[2] Although this was practically the situation in Scotland at that time, neither Mary nor Knox desired such a solution. The unity of the Church was sacrosanct. Nevertheless, in the mind of Knox, the unity of the crown and people in matters of religion was not the only possible form of social structure. Within the situation he saw only two possibilities.

The first was a return to the position which the Church held prior to the official recognition of the Christian religion in the Roman Empire. Knox declared that he was quite prepared to live under Mary as Paul had lived under Nero, although he had certain reservations.[3] Thus there can be seen ideas that have lately been brought into use by those who are aware of the advent of the post-Constantinian era.[4] The only difference being that Knox was prepared to identify Mary, if she remained a Roman Catholic, with the pagan rulers because of her adherence to the Antichrist, while today such a situation is seen as having arisen basically from the growth of secularism.

The second possibility Knox considered to be the only chance which appeared to be given of achieving reunification of crown and people within the faith. This could only be accomplished if Mary recognised the possibility of establishing a mutual contract between herself and her people. As he said, 'Therefore it shall be profitable to your Majesty, to consider what is the thing your Grace's subjects look to receive of your Majesty, and what it is that ye ought to do unto them by mutual contract. They are bound to obey you, and that not but in God, Ye are bound to keep laws unto them. Ye crave of them service: they crave of you protection and defence against wicked doers.'[5]

[1] *Inuentaires,* cxlvii.

[2] *Exhortation au Princes et Seigneurs du Conseil privé du Roi, pour obvier aux séditions qui semblent nous menacer pour le faict de la Religion.* Paris, 1561: cf. J. W. Allan, *op. cit.* 294.

[3] Knox, *History,* ii. 15.

[4] Prophetically described by G. Jacob, 'Die nachkonstantinische Situation', in *Für Arbeit und Besinnung.* Stuttgart, 1954. 226–42.

[5] Knox, *History,* ii. 72.

The idea of social compact or mutual contract was an appeal to authorities which each might have been prepared at least to honour. Here might be seen the reflection of Aristotle's concept of κοινωνία.[1] As he wrote 'friendly agreement is not about all things, but only about things that may be done by those in agreement or what relates to their common life'.[2] In Cicero's *Res Publica* he could of course have seen that it was in consent to law that the civil society was bound together.[3] Ideas such as these, which had been strong in the Middle Ages prior to the growth of the absolutist theories of the sixteenth century, continued in France. Knox was obviously fumbling after common ground. The confusion probably arose in this particular discussion because he was at that time concerned that Mary should implement certain acts of parliament and just because the problem was not faced in accordance with such constitutional ideas as those summarised by E. H. Kantorowicz in his study, *The King's Two Bodies*,[4] the search after an understanding completely disintegrated.

However, the problem raised its head again in another form when Mary asked at a subsequent meeting, 'what have ye to do with my marriage?'[5] which he had dared to criticise in spite of the approval given by the Cardinal of Lorraine,[6] and 'what are ye within the commonwealth?'[7] He took refuge in the theories of social compact or mutual contract—'A subject born within the same, Madam. And albeit I neither be Earl, Lord nor Baron within it, yet has God made me . . . a profitable member within the same: Yea, Madam, to me it appertains no less to forewarn of such things as may hurt it, if I foresee them, than it does to any of the Nobility'.[8]

It is significant to see that this doctrine, in fact, became to some extent public property after the marriage of Mary and Darnley in 1565 when the silver ryal was minted.[9] Inscribed upon the obverse of the coin were the words of the psalm, 'Let God arise

---

[1] Cf. the analysis of κοινωνία in *The Politics of Aristotle*, ed. W. L. Newman. Oxford, 1887, i. 41–44.

[2] *Ethica Eudemia*. 1241a.

[3] I, 26, 32.   [4] Princeton, 1957.

[5] Knox, *History*, ii. 82.

[6] *Calendar of State Papers, Foreign. Elizabeth*, ed. J. Stevenson. London, 1870, vii. 371, 401, 435.

[7] Knox, *History*, ii. 83.   [8] *Ibid.*

[9] E. Burns, *Coinage of Scotland*. Edinburgh, 1857, ii. 338–9.

F

and let his enemies be scattered'. This was in stark contradiction to the inscriptions which appeared on French coins lauding the King in great hyperbole.[1] The true message of the Scottish inscription can be gathered from the comments of John Calvin on this passage: 'There is much comfort to be derived from the circumstance, that those who persecute the Church are here spoken of as *God's enemies*. When he undertakes our defence, he looks upon the injuries done to us as dishonours cast upon his Divine Majesty.'[2]

Dickinson is right. 'Knox had believed that Church and State could be the twin pillars of God's house on earth: twin aspects of the government of God's people.'[3] What Knox was really striving after was not merely a mutual contract between sovereign and people but between Church and State, so that God's commonwealth would appear again in Scotland. As Percy puts it: 'there could be no more distinction between Church and realm, between civil government and divine purpose, than in Israel of old'.[4] Not only Mary 'but the worldly-wise rejected his godly policy as "devout imagination" '.[5]

The second accusation levelled by Mary against Knox was, as author of *The First Blast of the Trumpet against the Monstrous Regiment of Women*, Geneva, 1558, he had written a book against her authority. The place of women in society had been considered by Mary long before Knox's *First Blast* was published. In 1555, in the hall of the Louvre, she had delivered a public address in defence of learned women.[6] She had almost certainly been influenced by the humanist, Johannes Ludovicus Vives, a friend of Thomas More and Erasmus, whose book, *L'Institution de la femme*

[1] Kantorowicz, *Laudes Regiae*. 1–12.

[2] J. Calvin, *Commentary on the Book of Psalms*, trans. J. Anderson. Edinburgh, 1847, iii. 7.

[3] W. C. Dickinson, *The Scottish Reformation and its Influence upon Scottish Life and Character*. Edinburgh, 1960. 8.

[4] E. Percy, *John Knox*. London, 1935. 412.

[5] Dickinson, *op. cit.*

[6] The manuscript of which was still in her library (*Inuentaires*, cxiii). The address is referred to in the Latin dedication to Mary in A. Foclin de Chauny en Vermandois, *La rhetorique française*. Paris, 1555. Mary's address was probably based on Louis le Caron, *La claire, ou de la prudence de droit, dialogue premier. Plus, la clarté amoureuse*. Paris, 1554. The dialogue commences with the thesis that women are capable of learning, the practice of law and government.

chrétienne, Paris, 1553, may have been in her library.[1] The Queen of Scots, with a youthful eye on the English throne, was very sensitive to any ideological undermining of her authority in that connection as well as in Scotland. Her questions to Knox were: had she no just authority and did he speak of women in general?[2]

He was quite frank in admitting that *The First Blast* 'was written most especially against that wicked Jezebel of England':[3] most of the English Reformers had described Mary Tudor in this way.[4] In the course of the conversation, he revealed to Mary that he had not kept up his reading on this problem and it was clear that he was no longer greatly interested in the matter. He said, in fact, 'if the realm finds no inconvenience from the regiment of a woman, that which they approve shall I not further disallow than within my own breast, but shall be as well content to live under your grace as Paul was to live under Nero: and my hope is, that so long as that ye defile not your hands with the blood of the saints of God, that neither I nor that book shall either hurt you or your authority'.[5]

This change of attitude was quite significant and his later remarks to her appear to have suggested that he could safely forget the whole subject. 'It appeared to me that wisdom should persuade your Grace never to raise trouble for that which to this day has not troubled your majesty, neither in person yet in authority.'[6] Having said this, it is safe to say that Knox's attitude was in no way inspired, at least in this connection, by such thoughts as are expressed in an injunction given three hundred years later by Emerson, 'A foolish consistency is the hobgoblin of little minds, adored by little statesmen and philosophers and divines. With consistency a great soul has simply nothing to do. . . . Speak what you think now in hard words and to-morrow speak what to-morrow thinks in hard words again, though it contradict everything you said to-day.'[7]

[1] It depends on the doubtful identification (*Maitland Miscellany*, i. 7) of a translation of his *Instituione feminae Christianae*. Basel, 1538, as being in the library. Mary, however, would not have subscribed to his views on the restricted reading suitable for a Queen as set out in Book I.

[2] Knox, *History*, ii. 14–15.

[3] *Ibid.*, ii. 15.   [4] Cf. 69.

[5] Knox, *op. cit.*, ii. 15.   [6] *Ibid.*

[7] R. W. Emerson, *Essays*. First Series, new and revised ed. Boston, 1883. 58–59.

Yet, Knox's changes of emphasis caused more than a little mis-understanding, as some of what he said to Mary was in contrast to the teaching in *The First Blast*. In his book, he left practically no place for a female ruler in a lawful social order. He, to a slight extent, had kept a small door open when he admitted that 'God being free, may . . . dispense with the rigor of his law and may use his creatures at his pleasure',[1] but such exceptions as Deborah, although 'imbued with the spirit of wisdom, of knowledge, and of the true fear of God, and by the same she judged the facts of the rest of the people',[2] exercised a rule based on the use of 'the spiritual sword' and not on 'any temporal regiment or authority'.[3]

Since 1558, Knox's attitude had changed. He had moved nearer to Calvin's counsel which he had ignored when he had written his tract.[4] Calvin had not forgotten what he said and it was made clear to William Cecil, principal secretary to Elizabeth of England in January 1559, when he stated that 'There were occasionally women so endowed, that the singular good quality which shone forth in them, made it evident that they were raised up by divine authority: either that God designed by such example to condemn the activity of men or for the better setting forth of his glory. He brought forth Hulda and Deborah: and added, that God did not vainly promise by the mouth of Isaiah that queens should be the nursing mothers of the church: by which prerogative it is very evident that they are distinguished from females in private life.'[5]

As shown in the letter of Calvin and in Knox's remarks, there is an appreciation that the situation had changed, with a Protestant Queen on the throne of England in place of Bloody Mary and a delicate political situation in Scotland but yet one vastly different from the regime which ceased in England with the accession of Elizabeth.

It has to be remembered, in this context, that Knox still had hopes for the establishment of a new Commonwealth of Israel in Scotland. There may have been republican overtones,[6] it may

---

[1] Knox, *Works*, iv. 404.   [2] *Ibid.*, iv. 407–8.   [3] *Ibid.*, iv. 408.

[4] *The Zürich Letters*, Second Series, ed. H. Robinson. Parker Society, Cambridge, 1845. 34.

[5] *Ibid.* 34–35.

[6] H. Baron, 'Calvinist Republicanism and its historical Roots', in *Church History*. New York, 1939, viii. 30–42.

have had theocratic concepts similar to those of John Calvin,[1] Knox may have had certain reservations too, like Calvin,[2] about the place of the monarchy within the state,[3] nevertheless, this overriding concern for the Christian Commonwealth drove him to find a significant place for Mary within it should she ever be won for the Evangel.

It was the vividness of the onward-sweeping history of the chosen people reappearing in his day that fascinated him. Two female figures from the Old Testament epitomised for him the very antithesis of each other and represented for Knox the possible roles which Mary might play in Scotland. These were Jezebel and Deborah. Such a picture was not new. Some decades before, in Robert Henryson's *Orpheus and Eurydice*, Jezebel had appeared as one in hell along with Ahab.[4] To many, in the turbulence of the Reformation era, Jezebel and Ahab were considered to have reappeared in the form of Mary Tudor and Philip II.[5]

Jezebel was dead and Ahab was being kept at bay by the Protestant Queen of England. Was Mary now to become the Jezebel or would she be claimed for the Gospel and become the Deborah of Scotland? Knox was not over optimistic but, on leaving her presence for the first time, his final words to her were, 'I pray God, Madam, that ye may be as blessed within the Commonwealth of Scotland if it be the pleasure of God, as ever Deborah was in the Commonwealth of Israel'.[6]

Hopes of such a future soon vanished and it is not surprising to find Mary identified as Jezebel[7] and Delilah[8] in a ballad published in the early summer of 1567.

It was inevitable that the doctrine of the Mass should be raised in their discussions. It is interesting how little Knox has to say

[1] J. Bohatec, 'Zur Eigenart des "theokratischen" Gedankens bei Calvin', in *Festgabe für E. F. K. Müller*. Neukirchen, 1933. 122–57.

[2] W. Käser, 'Die Monarchie im Spiegel von Calvins Daniel-Kommentar', in *Evangelische Theologie*. Munich, 1951–52, xi. 112–37.

[3] Knox, *History*, ii. 120.

[4] *The Chepman and Myllar Prints. A Facsimile with a Bibliographical Note*, ed. W. Beattie. Edinburgh, 1950. 158.

[5] Cf. e.g., *Original Letters relative to the English Reformation*, ed. H. Robinson. Parker Society, Cambridge, 1847. 115.

[6] Knox, *History*, ii. 19–20.

[7] *Satirical Poems of the time of the Reformation*, ed. J. Cranstoun. Scottish Text Society, Edinburgh, 1891. 34, 36.

[8] *Ibid.* 32, 33.

to her, he tended merely to negate the beliefs of the church of Rome and made little reference to reformed doctrine apart from a vague general reference to Scripture. 'Take one of the chief points', he said, 'which this day is in controversy betwix the papists and us: for example, the Papists allege and boldly have affirmed, That the Mass is the ordinance of God, and the institution of Jesus Christ, and a sacrifice for the sins of the quick and the dead. We deny both the one and the other, and affirm that the Mass as is now used is nothing but the invention of man.'[1] He thereafter appeals to the Word of God and claims that 'Jesus neither said, nor yet commanded Mass to be said at his Last Supper, seeing that no such thing as their Mass is made mention of within the whole Scriptures'.[2]

Mary in reply merely claims that if Roman scholars were present they would answer him. She did not indicate how much she knew about the matter. She certainly could have learned a fair amount about Protestant doctrine from her own books for she had a copy of Calvin's *Institutes*[3] in French and Peter Martyr's book on the Lord's Supper.[4] It can be said that Mary's own attitude towards the Mass, apart from any political considerations which might have had an influence upon her, was doubtless confused. She was attracted by tradition and the spectacle of the Roman service yet, those, who by being with her in Scotland and who had made their views known, did not help her to clarify her mind. The priest, René Benoist, who came with her from France and was later to be dean of the theological faculty in Paris,[5] was concerned to achieve some kind of reconciliation in religious affairs. This can be seen in his book *Necessarius atque certus modus tollendae Religionis discordiae* (Paris, 1562), which was written in Edinburgh while in the Queen's service. A translation was later made by Ninian Winget, *Concerning Composing of Discords in Religion* (Paris, 1565). Mary had the Latin edition, together with three other volumes by Benoist.[6]

[1] Knox, *History*, ii. 18.   [2] *Ibid.*, ii. 19.
[3] *Inuentaires*, cxii.   [4] *Ibid.*
[5] E. Pasquier, René Benoist, le Pape de Halles (1521–1608). Paris, 1913.
[6] *Ibid.* i.e. *Le Triomphe et excellente victoire de la Foy, par le moyen de la véritable et toute puissante parole de Dieu*. Paris, 1562: *Traité du Sacrifice Evangelique*. Paris, 1564 and *Certaine resolution et détermination des points à présent controversés touchant la Religion Chrétien*. Paris, 1565.

On the other hand, her confessor, John Black, O.P., teacher in St Mary's College, St Andrews, was much more conservative, not only in his public activity but also in the theological position apparent from his surviving books and their marginalia.[1]

The ambivalence of Mary's attitude regarding the Mass is well illustrated in her having Ratramnus, *De Corpore et Sanguine Domini*.[2] Ratramnus had been a main source of influence on the Protestant view of the sacrament of the Lord's Supper held by Nicholas Ridley[3] and Thomas Cranmer.[4] An English translation had appeared as early as 1548, *The boke of Bartram Priest intreating of bodye and bloude of Christ* (London). Because of its teaching, it was considered by some to be a forgery by a heretic and was placed on the Index by Pope Paul IV in 1559 but its authenticity and orthodoxy have been accepted even by Roman scholars since the publication of the findings of Jean Mabillon. It is not possible to know from where this book came but it could have been a gift of her irenic priest, Benoist.

With such an insecure position, it is obvious that Mary was not prepared to listen to anything which Knox had to say about the Mass. She took refuge in a vague tradition rather than reveal her uncertainty.[5]

From what has been said, it will be obvious that it has only been possible to touch on two or three of the most obvious issues which created great differences of opinion between John Knox and Mary Stuart. Much remains to be investigated, in spite of the general opinion that this subject has been overdone.

To quote a most revered teacher Dr William Manson who wrote the following words in connection with his researches on the Epistle to the Hebrews, if I have ventured 'to take my rush-light afresh into some of the dark corners of this obscurity, it is with the consciousness that any illumination which I may hope to offer

[1] J. Durkan and A. Ross, *Early Scottish Libraries*. Glasgow, 1961. 10–11, 76.

[2] Cf. Ratramnus, *De Corpore et Sanguine Domini. Texte établi d'après les manuscrits, et notice bibliographique*, ed. J. N. Bakhuizen van den Brink. Amsterdam, 1954.

[3] *The Works of Nicolas Ridley, bishop of London*, ed. H. Christmas. Parker Society, Cambridge, 1841. 206.

[4] P. Brooks, *Thomas Cranmer's Doctrine of the Eucharist*. London, 1965. 41–43.

[5] Knox, *History*, ii. 19.

on this or that point may only cast into deeper shadow some untouched recesses of the problem. I hope it may not be so in the event, but the risk must be taken in an experiment of this kind, and I shall have to guard my taper-flame carefully against the wind, the more so as I am constrained to go in the teeth of certain opinions widely favoured at present and confidently offered as the introduction of a new and better hope for the understanding'[1] of this problem.

[1] W. Manson, *The Epistle to the Hebrews*. London. 1951. 8.

Delegates and Guests attending the Celebrations

The Right Rev. D. Abraham, The Hungarian Reformed Church in America.

Mr K. Albrecht, The University of Münster.

The Rev. Dr F. Ashton, The Congregational Union of Australia.

The Rev. Dr W. D. Bailie, The Presbyterian Church of Ireland.

Mr H. Bärend, The University of Münster.

The Rev. A. Boesak, The Dutch Reformed Mission in South Africa.

Landeskirchenrat Brinkmann, The United Church of Westphalia.

The Rev. H. L. Brownlie, The United Free Church of Scotland.

The Rev. J. Burke, The United Church of Canada.

The Rev. D. Campbell, The Free Presbyterian Church of Scotland.

The Rev. Te-Shieng Chang, The Presbyterian Church of Taiwan.

Mr T. L. Christensen, The University of Arhus.

Oberkonsistorialrat Class, The United Church of Berlin-Brandenburg.

The Rev. U. Dusse, The Reformed Synod of Denmark.

Kirchenpresident W. Ebrecht, The Protestant Evangelical Church of Pfalz.

The Rev. L. Erwin, The Presbyterian Church in the United States.

The Rev. Professor H. H. Esser, The University of Münster.

The Rev. Dr M. Gabriel, The Evangelical Church of the Union, German Democratic Republic.

Oberlandeskirchenrat D. Gang, The United Church of Kurhessen-Waldeck.

The Rev. J. Gatu, The Presbyterian Church of East Africa.

Oberkirchenrat W. Gerhard, The Evangelical Church of the Union, German Democratic Republic.

The Rev. Principal J. S. Glen, Knox College, Dunedin.

The Rev. R. Groscurth, The Evangelical Church of the Union, German Democratic Republic.

The Rev. Dr D. Herron, The Presbyterian Church in Canada.

The Rev. A. S. Horne, The Reformed Presbyterian Church of Scotland.

Mr S. Huang, The Presbyterian Church of Singapore and Malaysia.

The Right Rev. J. Huxtable, The United Reformed Church of England.

The Rev. M. Jinbashian, The Union of Armenian Evangelical Churches (N.E.).

Mr S. Kittler, The Evangelical Church of the Union, German Democratic Republic.

Mr J. L. P. von Scheffler-Knox, Hamburg.

The Rev. G. Koslowsky, The United Church of the Rhineland.

Bishop Dr F. Krummacher, The Evangelical Church of the Union, German Democratic Republic.

Mr D. M. Lloyd, The Presbyterian Church of Wales.

Kirchenrat B. Locher, The United Church of the Rhineland.

The Reverend Professor G. W. Locher, The University of Berne.

The Rev. Dr A. F. Luke, The Synod of the Nile of the Evangelical Church.

The Rev. President J. McCord, The Presbyterian Church of the United States.

The Rev. D. Macdonald, The Free Church of Scotland.

Mrs K. McFie, Edinburgh.

The Rev. D. Mafatlane, The Lesotho Evangelical Church.

Dr J. Matz, The Evangelical Church of the Union, German Democratic Republic.

Mr A. Mengel, The University of Münster.

The Rev. Professor G. E. Meuleman, The Reformed Churches in the Netherlands.

Miss E. Monzel, The University of Münster.

The Rev. H. Munro, The Presbyterian Church of Southern Africa.

The Rev. J. Mwape, The United Church of Zambia.

The Rev. T. Nagy, The Reformed Church of Hungary.

The Rev. Professor W. H. Neuser, The University of Münster.

The Rev. S. Noczana, The Church of Central Africa Presbyterian.

The Rev. A. J. Pieters, The Protestant Church of Belgium.

Mr W. Querl, The University of Münster.

The Rev. R. Ring, The Reformed Alliance, German Federal Republic.

The Rev. Dr J. Rogge, The Evangelical Church of the Union, German Democratic Republic.

Mr J. M. Ross, The United Reformed Church of England.

The Rev. Dr H. Russel, The Presbyterian Church in the United States.

The Rev. A. Sbaffi, The Waldensian Church.

The Rev. W. Schotanus, The London American Church.

Miss A. Schücking, The University of Münster.

Miss H. Schwarz, The University of Münster.

Mr J. J. Steenkamp, The University of Münster.

The Rev. R. Steward, The Reformed Church of France.

The Rev. W. H. Tanner, The Methodist Church in Scotland.

The Rev. J. I. Thomson, The Congregational Union of Scotland.

The Rev. Dr W. de Welder, The Church of Christ in China.

Mrs H. de Welder, The Reformed Church of America.

The Rev. W. Whyte, The Baptist Union of Scotland.

The Rev. Dr E. Wildbolz, The University of Berne.

The Rev. J. Wotherspoon, The Presbyterian Church in the United States.

The Rev. S. Yoshida, The Church of Christ in Japan.

The Rev. Professor G. Yule, The Presbyterian Church of Australia.

The Rev. R. M. Yule, The Presbyterian Church of New Zealand.

Index